The Delight
of
Being His Daughter

Dotty Schmitt

Logos International
Plainfield, New Jersey

All Scripture quotes, unless otherwise indicated, are from the King James Version.

Quotes marked RSV are from The Revised Standard Version, copyright © 1952, 1971 by the Division of Christian Education of The National Council of the Churches of Christ in the United States of America.

Quotes from The Amplified Bible are copyright © 1965 by Zondervan Publishing House.

Dedication

To the memory of my beloved dad, whose love and affection helped prepare me for the revelation of my heavenly Father's love, and to my precious husband, whose love and zeal for the Father continues to be the greatest inspiration in my pursuit of Him.

Contents

Foreword

It is a delight for me, as Dotty's husband, to write these few lines of foreword to this, the second edition of her book. Dotty is truly a remarkable lady, one who actually has that kind of honest walk with the Lord Jesus that these pages recount. Since I have been a first-hand observer of her life for over thirty years now (from the time I was a teenager in Brooklyn, New York), I can sincerely commend these chapters to the reader as the true story of a genuine woman of God. Indeed, "many daughters have done nobly, but you excel them all . . . a woman who fears the Lord, she shall be praised" (Prov. 31:29, 30).

Many have been the positive testimonies from those who have read this book in its original edition, and I am assured that this second edition will truly be a "second blessing" to the wider Body of our Lord Jesus Christ.

Dotty's husband, Charles P. Schmitt,*
Pastor, Immanuel's Church,
Silver Spring, MD
August 15, 1985

---

* Author of *Root Out of a Dry Ground,* a Church history, and *Our Tremendous Lover,* a devotional commentary on the Song of Songs.

Foreword to the Third Edition

Just an update! Exactly four years to the day have passed since the revised epilogue and the foreword to the second edition of this autobiography were written. These have been four of our most productive and blest years!

Laura Lea, our eldest daughter, graduated with her degree, is now married, and lives close by with her husband, George. Both are achievers in the field of computer science. Dianna Lynn graduated from Wheaton College with her degree and is working in a very responsible position as marketing director for the Agriculture Federal Credit Union in Washington, D.C. She presently works with the youth of Immanuel's Church. And Jenny Ann is now a happy **eighth** grader!

Dotty has her own daily radio program, "Joy of Discovery," and has just completed writing her latest book, **The Bride Wears Combat Boots.** Charles, one of the five pastors of Immanuel's Church, is also toying with writing another book of his own, **To Fly Again.**

In the spring of this Immanuel's Church dedicated its new worship center, which was full from the very first day it opened! Now in the fall of 1989, six months later, Immanuel's will be going to multiple services, seeking to accommodate the ever-growing, precious congregation of the Lord's people. Also, we hope that Phase Two of Immanuel's new worship center will soon be under construction. Like the prophet Samuel, we gratefully and humbly wish to raise our Ebenezer — "Hitherto hath the Lord helped us" (1 Samuel 7:12). Amen!

Charles and Dotty Schmitt
August 15, 1989

FOREWORD TO THE FOURTH EDITION

Nearly three and a half years have passed since the third edition of this autobiography. These have been some of our most productive and blest years. (I guess we said that in the foreword to the third edition! Well, it's still true!)

Now our dear Dianna Lynn is also married. She and her precious husband Scott live in Wheaton, Illinois. And Jenny Ann is now a happy *high schooler*!

Immanuel's Church has just continued to grow until we have run out of room in the areas of many of our most anointed activities. Plans for a new 2,400 seat auditorium with greatly expanded nursery and children's and youth areas is now on the drawing boards and construction will probably begin within a year and a half.

These are momentous days--as we live in the light of the dawning of the great Day of our God and the return of our beloved Lord Jesus! What a tremendous generation in which to serve the purposes of our God!

Charles & Dotty Schmitt
New Year's Day, 1993

Prologue

"Why did He always seem to be out to ruin my plans? Especially lately, it seemed that whatever exciting doors opened He closed them! What kind of God was I serving, anyhow?"

Impatiently I fumbled with my hall key, glad to be out of the hustle and bustle of New York City traffic for a while. Feeling miserable, I quickly ran up the one flight of stairs to our small, five-room apartment, hoping to escape to my little room for a brief respite.

"Why, just why, for once couldn't something work out the way I wanted it to?" Feeling suddenly guilty for my angry thoughts, I quickly tried to ignore them.

I finally got our apartment door opened and walked into our small, but comfortable living room. Mom was an immaculate housekeeper, and from the living room I could see the sun reflecting off the freshly polished kitchen floor. Good, no one was home! My dad was probably working on his meticulously kept car, and Mom was most likely out shopping. She would be kept pleasantly occupied talking to many of our neighbors, who would be sitting on the freshly swept and washed stoops. The homes were closely connected six-family houses that line the very busy, treeless thoroughfare of the German section of Gates Avenue. My brother Al was most likely out with his friends riding bikes or playing ball. Suddenly, I felt rather exhausted. As usual, I had commuted back and forth today, one hour each way, to the city college of Queens. But now, finally alone, I decided to forget the frustration and weariness of the past few hours.

I grabbed my Bible. I decided I would have "devotions" in my parents' bedroom instead, for there was more light there than in my own. Restlessly, I flipped through the pages. Nothing seemed to appeal to me. Every time I started reading a passage, I found my mind wandering to other thoughts. Maybe I should pray. Religiously, I knelt down beside my parents' bed, hoping somehow to impress God with my sincerity.

"Dear Lord, I thank Thee for Thy goodness and mercy. How great Thou art. Thou art righteous, and faithful . . ."

"Why aren't you honest with Me?"

"Because no religious God wants to hear what I'm really thinking or feeling."

"But I know it already. Remember the study you led on Psalm 139 in the small Inter-Varsity* prayer group on campus?"

"Yes, but what has that got to do with anything?" I turned in my Bible to this psalm and noticed verses 1-4:

O Lord, thou hast searched me, and known me.

*Inter-Varsity Christian Fellowship is a national evangelical organization for Christian students on college and university campuses in the United States.

Thou knowest my downsitting and mine uprising,
thou understandest my thought afar off.
Thou compasseth my path and my lying down, and art
acquainted with all my ways.
For there is not a word in my tongue, but, lo, O Lord,
thou knowest it altogether.

I slowly read, and reread, these verses.

"Well, Lord, I might as well be honest with You. It seems You already know how unspiritual my thoughts have been lately."

I paused, and as I quietly knelt on the carpetless floor of my parents' bedroom, I could almost feel the hand of God reaching deeply into my soul, bringing to the surface all the impurities of fear, unbelief, self-pity, and rebellion.

The tears began to flow freely from my embittered heart.

"God, I try to be spiritual. But deep down I guess I'm still afraid of You. I'm still afraid that You'll spoil my life. How do I know You won't send me to some miserable place to serve You? What about a future mate? Every time I become fond of someone, I sense You're there, saying no. O God, what are You really like? Help me, Father . . . *Father—Father?* Are You really my heavenly Father? Are You really more concerned for me than my beloved earthly dad? . . . *Dad*—can I truly call *You* Dad?"

As my mouth spoke these words, I experienced a warm inner cleansing. And even more startling at the moment was the suddenly clear revelation that broke upon my understanding. God was my *Father.* So this is what Paul meant when he wrote:

For ye have not received the spirit of bondage again to fear; but ye have received the Spirit of adoption, whereby we cry, Abba, Father. The Spirit [himself] beareth witness with our spirit, that we are the children of God. (Rom. 8:15-16)

Father, thank You that it's been a delight learning to be Your daughter.

And so the following pages shall serve to unfold to my readers the delightful and happy (but sometimes painful) adventure which has been mine of being His daughter.

THE DELIGHT OF
BEING HIS DAUGHTER

1

The Day the Sun Shone

For the Lord is a sun and shield: the Lord will give grace and glory: no good thing will he withhold from them that walk uprightly.

(Ps. 84:11)

"Come on, you don't want us to be late, do you?" Arlene asked, as she tried to wait patiently for me.

Leaning against our newly purchased washing machine, which sat against the wall between our two large, sparkling-clean kitchen windows, I strained to get a better look at the freshly applied lipstick I was wearing. This was the first time I was allowed to use lipstick. My heart skipped a beat with the excitement of the day. As I whirled away from the mirror, I could feel the lengthy soft material touch my ankles. My first long dress! This was more thrilling than I had anticipated!

Finally putting on my long white gloves, I glanced up to see Arlene frown.

"OK, OK, I'm almost ready."

"Now don't be late!" I called to my folks. "And make sure the family all gets to sit in the front pews." Arlene and I were making our way quickly down our apartment stairs as I yelled back to my parents. This was one of the biggest days of my life. Dad had baked—in his uniquely artistic way—a huge cake beautifully resembling a

1

large family Bible. And Tante Erna and Uncle Walter had decked out their lovely home for the afternoon activities. A gala family dinner would be served with the many fine trimmings. All my aunts, uncles, and cousins would be there. I could hardly wait. I guess all the tedious weeks of boring catechism class were worth this one big day!

The sun shone brilliantly through the multicolored stained-glass windows. As a group of us twelve-year-olds marched solemnly down the aisle of the elegant, gothic-like church edifice, I began to experience the love of God for the first time I could consciously remember. Sitting there in the church pew, with the sun warmly and almost piercingly shining down upon me, I *knew* God was alive and that somehow He had a purpose for my life.

The big confirmation day passed with much traditional celebration and excitement. In the midst of the activity, the presence of God passed from my consciousness, but only for a season—because He who was to become the very Sun of my soul had begun to touch my life actively with His penetrating love.

For many years after this eventful day, I found myself pondering the meaning of the first article of the Westminster Catechism: "What is the chief end of Man? The chief end of Man is to glorify God and to enjoy Him forever." How could anyone know God, let alone *enjoy* Him? The words *"enjoy God"* seemed to have been burnt with a hot iron upon my heart. Little did I realize that before me lay the great adventure of not only getting to know my God but of also getting to thoroughly enjoy Him who was to become the Light of my life.

Thank You, Father, for being to us—Your children—the blessed "Hound of Heaven." And thank You for the warmth of Your presence which melts the coldness of our hearts.

2

Evening of Encounter

*Ye have not chosen me, but I have chosen you,
and ordained you, that ye should go and bring
forth fruit, and that your fruit should remain.*

(John 15:16)

"Say, would you close the one button on the back of
my blouse?" Cathy turned whispering to me as I sat behind her in our seventh-grade class of P.S. 93, Queens.
I liked Cathy. She had short, shining black hair, and her
eyes sparkled with laughter. After Mrs. Wortman finished dictating the spelling words to us, Cathy turned to
me again.

"How would you like to come with me tonight to a
great youth group?"

"Well, I don't know. Where is it?"

"In the basement of Trinity Reformed."

"Trinity Reformed? Why that's my church! I didn't
know you went there. I thought you were Catholic!"

"Yeah, well, I am Catholic, but I go there too. You want
to come?" She really had me curious now. What was a
Catholic girl doing going to a Protestant church, and *my*
church at that?

"Yeah, sure, since it's in my church, I'm sure my folks
will let me go."

Even though the youth group was held in my church

3

basement, I was surprised to see so many young people whose faces were unfamiliar to me. I did know Dotty Korff—one of the smartest girls in the seventh grade—from confirmation class and from school. So she and Cathy sat with me when the meeting began.

Our pastor's daughter, Anna, got up to speak to the group after we finished singing a few songs. She used a flannelgraph board to illustrate the death and resurrection in the life of Christ.

"God so loved the world, that he gave his only begotten Son, that whosoever believeth in him should not perish, but have everlasting life." Anna quoted frequently from this John 3:16 verse. Even though I had gone to Sunday school since I was five, and had recently been confirmed, what Anna was saying seemed brand-new to me.

"Jesus so loved you that He died for your sins. . . . Have you received Him; have you accepted God's great gift to you? . . . Do you personally know that Jesus Christ is alive?"

My heart began to pound within me as Anna brought her little message to a close.

"Is there anyone here who wants to receive Jesus Christ as their personal Savior?" Anna asked.

Why was I feeling so strange? There was that same warm feeling I had first felt on confirmation day. Why was my heart pounding so much?

"If you have never before personally accepted Jesus into your life, simply raise your hand and ask Him to come into your life. Remember, Jesus himself says in Rev. 3:20, 'Behold, I stand at the door, and knock: if any man hear my voice, and open the door, I will come in to him, and will sup with him, and he with me.' " And then Anna waited for us to respond. My arm felt as if it weighed fifty pounds, but finally I put it up. As my hand

4

went up, for the first time in my life I knew that Jesus had died for my sins. I knew that by His blood He bought back my soul from sin. Yes, I now knew for myself that Jesus Christ was not just a Sunday-school-story figure; He was my risen Savior.

Cathy and Dotty could not hide their exuberance about my decision to receive Jesus. They had apparently also recently made the same discovery about Jesus I had that night. In fact, all of these young people appeared to have a special "aliveness" about them. I soon learned that this youth group in the Trinity Reformed church basement consisted of young teens from many other churches who had all had the same salvation experience.

From among them all was one fourteen-year-old who to me especially stood out. He got up to speak a few words after Anna finished sharing. He was already quite tall for his age, and had strikingly big, dancing brown eyes. His hair was dark brown with a slight wave in it, and his face was handsomely expressive.

"You all know from Romans 3 that *all* have sinned, and *all* have fallen short of God's glory! Therefore, it's our obligation to preach the gospel to everyone. First to those in Jerusalem, then to those in Judea, then in Samaria, and finally to those in the uttermost parts of the world," he quoted from the book of Acts (1:8).

"Our school is our Jerusalem. Our neighborhood is our Judea. How will they believe unless someone tells them the message? Is your Bible on top of your books? Do you have a generous supply of good salvation tracts to hand out? Remember that Paul said, in Rom. 1:16: 'I am not ashamed of the gospel of Christ: for it is the power of God unto salvation to every one that believeth; to the Jew first, and also to the Greek.' "

I slouched back down into my chair as this young man

continued to preach fervently to us about our witness to the world. He didn't seem to be reading from a prayer. How did he know all this stuff? And what was Romans and Acts? And what did Jerusalem have to do with my school? As my mind tried to figure out all he was saying, I seemed to understand his spirit more than his words. What an unusual and zealous young man! There was undoubtedly a spiritual fire burning within him for the Lord. I couldn't help but wonder who he was.

After the meeting, Cathy went over to this young man and asked him to come meet someone who had just found the Lord. Enthusiastically he bounced across the room, and in a flamboyant manner took my hand, kissed it, and welcomed me to Trinity Youth Fellowship. And that was the way I first met Charlie. For the second time that night I was sure everyone could hear my heart pound within me. Who was this most unusual and attractive young man?

Already the delicate fingers of the great Potter were at work in the molding of my life. For not only had I met Him who was the Way, the Truth, and the Life that early spring evening in New York, but I had also met the one, who—in another twelve and a half years—would become my beloved husband.

How amazing, Father, that even before we were born, You knew our names, and chose a path for us to walk in! How great is Your plan of redemption!

To Burn as a Clinker or a Coal?

*So then because thou art lukewarm, and neither
cold nor hot, I will spue thee out of my mouth.*

(Rev. 3:16)

"What's your favorite verse, Dotty?" asked our Hi.
B.A.* leader. Quickly I tried to think of the passage
Cathy had often quoted: "Call unto me, and I will answer
thee, and shew thee great and mighty things, which
thou knowest not" (Jer. 33:3). I was surprised I could
quote it. It had been two years since I had given my heart
to the Lord, but my personal life hadn't changed very
much. It was great going to the youth group, and to Hi.
B.A. after school. I really enjoyed being with the other
kids. But when I was home alone, I still felt somewhat
empty. A lot of the other kids appeared to enjoy reading
the Scriptures, but I still couldn't get interested. The
Bible was so hard for me to understand that I was happy
if I could at least pronounce the names of the books in it.

"What's that all over your face and hands?" one of the
kids in school asked me for the umpteenth time. You'd
think I'd get used to that type of question by now, having

---

*Hi. B.A. stands for High School Born-Againers, an evangelical
Christian high school organization.

had severe eczema since I was but a couple of months old. But everything was worse since I'd become a teenager. The questions from other kids cut me a little more deeply, and the turmoil as to why *I* had to have this icky stuff all over me now became a whirlwind of confusion inside of me.

In fact, becoming a Christian had increased my inner conflicts. "Surely, God, You will heal me now that I'm a believer. O God, please heal me." Often I'd cry myself to sleep at night sobbing this prayer to God. During the past two years, rather than getting better, my physical condition got worse. A feeling of bitterness was growing within me. Secretly I would think, "My dad has spent literally thousands of dollars on me trying to get some answer for this problem; now what kind of God would sit idly by and not answer the prayers of His children?" I could cope with my turmoil and growing disillusionment as long as I was with my other Christian friends. When they quoted Scripture and prayed, it helped. To me, though, the Bible was a closed book. To pray when I was alone was an absolute bore. And yet how desperately I needed the support of these Christian teen-agers. Their prayers for me, and their total acceptance of me even when I looked terrible, felt soothing to my insides, even as the daily application of the hot oils and ointments felt to my skin on the outside.

"Dotty, we've just had a prayer meeting, and we're taking a stand on your healing." The familiar voice of Charlie came emphatically through the phone receiver. Since I had missed another day of school because my face, arms, and legs were so badly broken out, the kids decided to meet after school for special prayer at Elizabeth's house.

"Healing?" I responded weakly. As Charlie enthusiastically quoted Scripture to me, and tried to encourage me to take a "real stand of faith," an inner feeling of dread began to take hold of me. "Oh, no," I thought, "what if it doesn't work? Then what will I do?"

"And anyhow, we're so sure of this healing that we've set next Tuesday by four o'clock as the deadline for it." By the time Charlie finished speaking, my dread changed to a growing anticipation. Could it really be that God would heal me by next Tuesday at four o'clock?

On my hanging up the phone, my depression of the past day vanished. Dad had just gotten up from trying to get some sleep during the day, since he worked as an A & P night foreman in the large bakery division in Queens.

"Mom, Dad, guess what? That was the kids from the youth group. They've been praying, and guess what? I'm going to be healed!" My dad slowly put down his coffee cup. With his usual, quiet intensity he fixed his large brown eyes soberly on me.

"Dotty, you're crazy. This religious nonsense has got to stop. Martha, I told you to keep her away from those crazy meetings."

"But, Daddy, it's really going to happen. In fact, it's going to happen by four o'clock next Tuesday afternoon." With this, my dad stood to his full frame of five feet six inches, and scowled at me.

"Dotty, things don't happen like that. You've got to be normal. God doesn't work like that. He helps those who help themselves."

Hadn't Charlie told me to confess my faith? If I talked often about my being healed, wouldn't God know that I was really moving in faith? Yet all the while that I was so boldly proclaiming my faith, inner doubts kept nagging at me.

Not being able to hide his complete exasperation with me, Dad finally left the apartment to work on his car.

9

"But, Mom, you believe me, don't you?" As often happened, Mom was emotionally torn between Dad's skepticism and my verbal expression of fervor and faith.

That night I could hardly sleep. I kept thinking of all the clothes I could afterwards wear when I was healed which I could not wear with eczema all over me. Maybe now I could put on something other than blouses with long sleeves and high necks. Boy, what a relief *that* would be to Mom—not having to wash, starch, and iron those stupid long-sleeve blouses anymore. With thoughts of new clothes filling my mind, I finally fell asleep.

That week the young people frequently met for prayer. They kept pumping me full of Scriptures about healing. If *they* were so convinced I would be healed, God should at least be a little impressed. The only one who seemed somewhat quiet and sobered about all of this was our Hi. B.A. leader. He sure was a neat guy. Yet in the midst of all our fervor, he kept interjecting Scriptures on the will of God.

When Tuesday came we were all full of expectancy. My dad became quieter with each passing day. I got home from school at three-fifteen, and went alone into my room to pray. The kids thought this would be the thing for me to do. The clock seemed to be standing still. Finally it was four o'clock!

"Thank You for healing me," I said with as convincing a tone of voice as I could produce. It was now four-fifteen! I looked at my hands and arms. No change! I called Charlie, and the young people who were again gathered to pray.

"Well, what went wrong?"

"Nothing, just continue to stand in faith," Charlie replied.

That night we had to go someplace as a family. In

order to prove my faith, I chose to wear a beige, short-sleeve woolen dress. Wool was normally something I had to keep a five-foot distance from.

"Now God would surely be impressed by my bold demonstration of faith," my mind reasoned.

I returned home that night with my skin so irritated that I could hardly stand it. My dad sighed both in anger at me and in hurt for me.

"Dotty, now you know you've gone overboard. You know people can get crazy from too much religion. You can believe, but you still have got to remain normal." He was still speaking as I sulked off to go to bed. It was almost impossible to sleep. The disappointment I felt was the deepest I had ever known.

"I knew underneath all along that I'd never be healed. He couldn't be a loving God. Certainly if I were a parent I'd do all I could if my child were sick. What a deception." And so my mind kept brooding until, in mental and physical exhaustion, I finally fell asleep.

The days and weeks immediately ahead proved to be the most miserable period of my life.

"There's just nothing more we seem to be able to do for her, Mr. Fricker. All we've tried either irritates her condition more, or only very slightly relieves it," one of the leading dermatologists in Brooklyn sympathetically informed my dad and myself. "Perhaps a total change of climate would help. Maybe Florida would be an answer," he continued. My physical condition had definitely gotten worse the past couple of weeks, as well as my emotional depression.

Our youth group remained comparatively undaunted by "the test of faith" in regard to my healing. My attitude became more and more bitter, and soon my words revealed what was going on in my heart.

"I don't believe in anything any more. It's just all a bunch of mumbo jumbo anyhow," I responded to my friend Jeanie's quoting of Scripture to me. "Just leave me alone, will you? My dad said you screwballs are going to drive me crazy and I m beginning to believe it," I screamed one afternoon at one of the fellows from the youth group. Even though I yelled angrily to be left alone, my heart ached for their attention and friendship.

In absolute misery, I left for Florida in the middle of the school year with my parents and a neighbor friend. My dad had converted the back of his well-kept Hudson into a bed for me. We left on our trip to Florida with my body bandaged and my spirit so bruised that I didn't much care what happened next.

It was years later, as I sat with a friend in a little farmhouse in northern Minnesota, that the Lord revealed to me what had actually taken place in those months.

"What are you putting into your stove?" I asked Virginia.

"This is a clinker," Virginia replied. "Even though it looks like a coal, it isn't. Clinkers only burn when they're with other coals."

"And that's what you were at one time in your life, My daughter. You could only glow when you were with other Christians." My heart responded knowingly to the voice of my heavenly Father that cold winter evening in the Minnesota backwoods. Many years had now passed since those dismal teen experiences, many good, exciting and challenging years!

Thank You, Father, for not getting discouraged with us. Your patience is overwhelming at times. Thank You for not allowing us to remain in the dreadful state of lukewarmness. Yes, Father, You've called us to be coals and not clinkers.

4

The Dawning of a New Day

Can a woman forget her sucking child, that she should not have compassion on the son of her womb? yea, they may forget, yet will I not forget thee. Behold, I have graven thee upon the palms of my hands.

(Isa. 49:15-16)

"And, dear Lord, please remember Dotty. Bring her back to Yourself. Convict her of her backslidden condition."

Smugly I stood in the back of the Sunday school room listening to Charlie and the other kids praying. How ironic that I should walk in just when they were praying for me.

We had just gotten back from Florida. No one really knew I was back yet. One of my aunts felt I needed a "lift," and so she bleached my hair a golden blonde. My physical condition had improved some, but my spiritual and emotional state had definitely become worse.

Standing in the back of the Sunday school room with my blonde hair piled on top of my head, my eyes heavy with eye makeup, and my ears tingling with the weight of the long gold earrings I was wearing, I snickered to myself. "Wait till they see what their prayers have accomplished."

"Hi, gang!"

They all turned, and, while obviously a little stunned

14

at my appearance, came forward to warmly welcome me home—except for one, who upon seeing me, put his face in his hands and groaned, "Oh, no!"

"Good for him," I privately thought. "Now at least Charlie knows how useless all this praying is."

Spring passed into summer, summer into fall, and soon the Christmas season of 1954 was upon us. I had just turned "miserable" fifteen. The past months seemed to drag by. School was a chore—and a bore—to me. Only my friends seemed to give me any semblance of happiness.

"How long will life continue this way?" I found myself often inwardly questioning. I hadn't really prayed or read the Bible in months. That, I had decided, was simply a crutch for weak people.

With the Christmas season came also a very serious complication in my physical condition. Somehow I had not only gotten a very serious outward infection, but this time my whole insides became infected as well. For three weeks I lay in bed with a high fever, painful boils covering the top half of my body. The inner rebellion which had been seething for so many months burned itself out during those painful weeks, and left but the ashes of a desperate and aching heart.

My parents allowed only some of my closest girlfriends to come visit me.

"Since you can't answer me back now, I'm going to pray for you, and read some Scripture that the Lord gave me for you," Jeanie gently but firmly told me one afternoon. My face was covered with little tiny boils so that I could eat only by putting a straw through my lips. "I don't understand why God is allowing this, Dotty, but I know He loves you, and He has His hand on your life," Jeanie continued. Tears fell from my closed eyes. Oh

God, how desperately I wanted to believe that!

How well I could identify with David's complaint: "My days are like a shadow that declineth; and I am withered like grass" (Ps. 102:11). It was now that the Potter's hand moved with a most decisive stroke.

Our German cuckoo clock, which hung impressively on our living room wall, struck five times. I had been restless the whole night. Suddenly the room in which I lay seemed to become electric with the presence of One whom I only slightly knew.

"My child, what have you done for Me?" It seemed as if I were standing in the presence of One who was clothed in dazzling brightness. Somewhat shielding my eyes from the tremendous light, I tremblingly responded, "O God, if You give me my life back whole, I will serve You all the days I live." He responded to my words by literally filling me with the warmth of His love from the crown of my head to the soles of my feet. I lay there on my bed, on that cold winter morning, simply basking in His presence.

"Jesus loves me! this I know, For His Spirit tells me so," my heart began to sing over and over again in those early morning hours. "He loves me; God loves me just as I am; He totally accepts me. If He so loves and accepts me, I no longer have to work so hard to try to be accepted by other people. He truly *accepts* me as I am in His Beloved Son." Like a cleansing fire, these thoughts swept over my spirit.

"Dad, He is alive, I'm going to be OK. Please, Dad, put on Mario Lanza's record, 'I'll Walk with God'; I just want to hear the words." Patiently Dad listened to my words that eventful morning, and quietly put the record on for me. All that day, Mom and Dad lovingly served me. I sensed they knew something had happened, but as Dad verbalized a number of months later, he wasn't sure if I was delirious from the fever or had actually crossed over the brink into a general breakdown.

Within three weeks I returned to school a completely transformed individual. My entire personality was changed. Since I now knew by His Spirit and His Word that I was completely *accepted* in the Beloved (Eph. 1:6), how could I not accept myself? If He loved me regardless of what I looked like or even felt like, then He was the source of my acceptability and security. Whereas before I was very much the follower and never the leader in anything, I now found that the initiative for many projects was springing out of the zeal He had placed within my heart for himself. Most amazing of all was the mental awakening which took place. When Jesus filled me with His life, it was as if He also swept away all the cobwebs from my mind. Intellectually I became alive, and for the first time I actually enjoyed learning. My school average went from a 72 the previous term to a 94 the next. (Since I had never seriously entertained the thought of college, it did not dawn on me then that had I continued with 70 averages the city colleges would have been closed to me. But again the Potter knew His intent for this particular vessel, and also knew that averages in the 90s during the remaining high school terms were expedient for college entrance requirements.)

Perhaps most significant of all which transpired in my life spiritually during those days was the growing desire to know His Word. The Scriptures were no longer unintelligible but were now food to my hungry soul. How aptly David was able to describe this longing of the heart for the Word of the Lord: "More to be desired are they than gold, yea, than much fine gold: sweeter also than honey and the honeycomb" (Ps. 19:10).

Although the physical healing was to be a process, I

17

soon learned the truth of Prov. 4:20-22: "My [daughter], attend to my words; incline thine ear unto my sayings. Let them not depart from thine eyes; keep them in the midst of thine heart. For they are life unto those that find them, and health to all their flesh."

"Dorothy, you are to march in with the first third of the class," Miss Bowden, the dean of girls, told me as we began to line up for graduation night. My heart began to beat faster. That meant I was to get some kind of graduation award. How pleased Mom and Dad would be! Before the evening ended I had received not only one but four graduation awards. The most significant one for me was the school government award. Totally unaware of the impact my actions were having on the teachers, I had been very diligently attempting to help problematic students by befriending them and counseling them. God had made such a difference in my needy life that I had no doubt He could also help them. And for this endeavor I had received the school government award, along with the three other awards. Mom and Dad beamed. These past four years had been rough on all of us, but how gracious the Potter's hand had been!

It was also with a tinge of sadness that I graduated from Grover Cleveland High School. I would deeply miss the comradeship of our youth group. We had been about thirty strong in high school and our commitment to the Lord and to one another had made itself known to many at the school. I now chuckled as I recalled how Charlie had stationed us at every staircase so that we could hand out tracts to all the students when the bell rang. How thrilled we all were when Charlie, Dave, or Vic gave an altar call in the Martin Luther Club in school one afternoon. Boldly we would hold street meetings, telling others about Jesus. And frequently the teachers would find their letter boxes filled with gospel tracts.

Again, one among us seemed especially to stand out for his zeal and fervor for the Lord. His aptness in the teaching of the Scriptures, even as a teen-ager, now more than ever before captivated my heart. When he graduated from high school one year ahead of me and went off to attend a Bible school some three thousand miles from New York, I knew he had captured a unique yet undefined place in my heart.

Father, will we ever be able to really grasp the depth of Your love? How incredible that our names should be written upon the palms of Your hands! Thank You that You can lead us and guide us in Your paths from early age.

5

It's Time to Swim, Daughter

*Afterward he measured a thousand; and it was
a river that I could not pass over: for the waters
were risen, waters to swim in, a river that could
not be passed over*

(Ezek. 47:5)

"So what do you think?" my friend Dotty asked me.
"Think? Think about what?" I coyly asked her.
"Bill, silly; you know what I'm talking about.'
"Oh, Dotty, I'm so excited. Yes, he asked me to the
Inter-Varsity Christmas banquet. It sure took him long
enough." Dotty and I hugged one another and skipped
around the room in typical seventeen-year-old abandon.
My first formal affair—and with Bill! How great! Dotty's
special friend, Victor, had introduced me to Bill. They
were both attending Queens College, the school Dotty
and I would ourselves soon be attending, and both appeared so very intellectual and mature. What new adven-
tures lay ahead of me! It was so great to be alive!

Through those early college days my friendship with
Bill grew. He provided an intellectual challenge which
opened many new vistas for me. As the months pro-
gressed Bill was becoming more and more a part of my
life. Many times in my diary I would write, "Oh, Lord,
please tell me. What is Your will for Bill and myself?"
Increasingly I looked forward to the times he and I would

spend together talking and challenging one another on various points of Christian doctrine. He was a committed Lutheran, in doctrine, and I, a committed fundamentalist.

"You simply get too emotional and subjective about Christianity," Bill would say. "You talk about Jesus," he continued, "as if He were your own personal bar of ivory soap. You remind me of 'the schwarmerish movement' during the Reformation whom Luther said 'swallowed the Holy Ghost, feathers and all'."

"Oh yeah?" I countered. "Well you remind me of some cold objective theologian hiding away with his theology and philosophy books in an ivory tower someplace." And so our discussions would frequently come alive with quite different approaches to Christianity.

At first it was amusing and stimulating, but as Bill began to win more and more of a place in my heart and affections, our differences began to disturb me. One day as I shared my dilemma with Dotty and Vic, Vic simply turned to me and quoted from Amos 3:3: "Can two walk together, except they be agreed?" Even though I "chuckled the verse off" as not being relevant to two people who were actually believers, it nonetheless pierced like a spear into my spirit. I really enjoyed being with Bill, and with all our mutual friends. We were believers, and that's all that mattered at the time. Besides, I was beginning to suspect that I really was in love with Bill. More and more I would find myself wondering what marriage would be like, and what the Lord had in His mind for me.

It was in the midst of some of these thoughts that the Lord began to speak to me from His Word. My devotional studies were taking me through the Psalms. One evening as I was meditating upon Psalm 73, verses 25 and 26 were especially quickened to me: "Whom have I in heaven but thee? and there is none upon earth that I desire beside thee. My flesh and my heart faileth: but God is the strength of my heart, and my portion for ever." Quite spontaneously I echoed these words enthusiastically in prayer before the Lord: "You are indeed everything to me, Lord."

As I prayed, I heard a still, small voice ask, "Do you really mean these words, My daughter?"

"Why of course, Lord; how could You even ask?"

"Are you willing to go through life single if this be *My* will for you?"

Who popped the bubble? I immediately rebuked the devil; and when that didn't work, I was sure that the still, small voice was but the workings of my own aesthetic imaginings. Needless to say, devotions came to an abrupt end that night, and I quickly went to bed with the assurance that I would awaken feeling quite differently.

Upon awakening I decided to "devote" in another area of Scripture. The "river" which had arisen as a result of my meditation of Psalm 73 was just a little too deep for me to be comfortable in. For the next few days the Lord and I were on friendly but rather distant terms. Strangely enough, I found my joy somewhat ebbing, and in my mind I was constantly trying to block out the encounter He and I had had over this Psalm. Finally, one night I could bear the strain no longer. "Look, Lord, I feel You asked a very unfair question the other night. You know how very much I want eventually to be married. After all, *You* made me that way!" Again I looked at the particular passage which was now causing me such consternation: "Whom have I in heaven but thee? *and there is none upon earth that I desire beside thee.*" Oh (groan), Lord, must I swim this river?

Without a doubt I knew this river could not simply be bypassed; I had to face the issue squarely and honestly.

Was Jesus my supreme satisfaction in heaven *and on earth*? If He called me to a life of service as a single person, could I trust Him to satisfy my every need? For days I wrestled with this issue in His presence—and out of it. At last, one night I came exhaustedly before Him: "Lord, quite honestly I can't say yes to this question, but I know enough about You to be assured of Your perfect love towards me. I know—at least in my head—that Your will is good, acceptable, and perfect; therefore, Lord, *You* make me willing: I am willing to be made willing." Instantly the joy of the Lord returned, and the strain between Him and me disappeared.

Weeks passed without my giving too much further thought to the issue of Psalm 73. But one evening as I was worshiping before Him, He again asked the key question; and to my own amazement, I wept the answer affirmatively before Him. The miracle of grace had again worked deeply within my soul. Yea, Lord, *Thy will be done!* By the deep and unconscious workings of His grace and mercy, this river had also been swum across! He again had revealed another aspect of His character to me: His all-sufficiency. A new confidence was born within me towards Him. I could trust Him with my future. He knew all about Bill, and if we allowed Him to, He would absolutely provide the best for each of us in this life. "It's OK, Lord, You're my first priority. I'm willing to be single or married. Just You direct my life."

Father, with the skill and precision of a surgeon's hands, You're able to find the exact source of that which hinders our growth in You. Thanks, Father, for not allowing us to deceive ourselves about the depth of our devotion to You when in actuality it's really quite shallow. And also, thanks for not being satisfied until we've learned to swim in the ocean of Your love.

6

A Dark Night

For thou wilt light my candle: the Lord my God will enlighten my darkness. For by thee I have run through a troop; and by my God have I leaped over a wall. As for God, his way is perfect: the word of the Lord is tried: he is a buckler to all those that trust in him.

(Ps. 18:28-30)

"And so Camus virtually fulfilled his philosophy of life. Yesterday his sports car ran off the road in France and he was killed at the height of his intellectual career. The 'basis of life is tragic,' wrote the secular existentialists, and so Camus seems to have proven his thesis to the world." Thus did one of the leading professors of the philosophy department at Queens College emotionally inform his class. Dr. Woolf had been a student of the French existentialist Albert Camus, and was obviously moved by the absurdity of his untimely end. "Of course, Miss Fricker would have a different explanation of his death. Most likely, according to your philosophy of life, Miss Fricker, this would all be part of God's will," Dr. Woolf smilingly addressed me. There was a mutual respect between us, student and professor, even though we were worlds apart in our "Weltanschauung."* We had already had many interchanges as to the philosophical validity of the Christian faith. And even though he

---

*The German expression for philosophy of life.

24

thoroughly disagreed with my point of view, I knew he respected my position. What he did not know that morning after Camus' death was the terrible intellectual struggle I was presently experiencing.

I was thoroughly enjoying college, and found the intellectual stimulation very exhilarating. One professor especially, Dr. McDermott, from the same philosophy department, had a very strong influence upon me, and upon the direction my college studies were to take.

"Can you believe the richness of life that was restored to the human being during the period of the Enlightenment? People could read, learn, study, experiment, discover, create! A whole new era was being ushered in." With great enthusiasm, Dr. McDermott was able to inspire the freshman contemporary civilization class to want also to learn, study, and create. Mainly through his enthusiasm as a philosophy teacher, I found myself wanting to further pursue studies in the realm of philosophy.

Little did I realize how these studies would affect my Christian walk. Increasingly I found myself more and more defensive in regard to the claims of Christianity. That morning as Dr. Woolf gave me the opportunity to give a Christian interpretation to the absurdity of Camus' death, I knew my response was intellectually weak and philosophically very unconvincing.

What if William James were right in his *Varieties of Religious Experience?* What if there *were* many good roads which all led to the same God? And what about the unusual religious experiences many of these people had had who made no claim to believe solely in Jesus Christ? How could I be so sure that I was right to believe that in the midst of these numerous religions, Christianity alone was true and right? Wasn't I holding a very naive and intellectually untenable position?

These questions and many more plunged me into a terrible mental confusion, and resultant spiritual darkness.

"This is absolutely stupid," I reasoned with myself one day as I was emotionally defending Christianity to a fellow student. "If I were really secure as a Christian, I certainly wouldn't have to defend so adamantly Jesus Christ." I soon realized that the insecurity of my faith was what was causing me to be so loudly defensive.

"Look, Lord, You either are or You aren't. I know I've had a number of traumatic religious experiences, but so have other people who never have claimed to be Christians. So what I'm saying is, if You are really there, and if You, Jesus, are the *only* Way to the Father, You've got to show me. Because if You're not, I'm going to find something else to throw my life and energies into."

With a sigh of relief I jumped off my bed where I had made this little verbal transaction with God. Before I could leave my small bedroom, though, I was apprehended by a still, small voice speaking inside of me: "There is only one Book which I have uniquely claimed as My own. Read it, as you would your history or philosophy books; read it diligently each day."

"OK, Lord, if that's really Your voice speaking, and if that's part of the agreement, I'll consistently read it each day."

One of the experiences which had thus far caused me so thoroughly to enjoy my college days was my involvement in the Inter-Varsity Christian Fellowship on campus. We were a small group, but an intellectually alive and spiritually hungry one. Only God knows what would have happened to me as a Christian had I not had the support of that handful of dedicated believers. A few of them knew of the anguish I was experiencing during those days. Very wisely they did not preach to me, but simply believed with me that I would find the answers I was looking for. How gratefully I now recall the time we spent together studying the Gospel of John and the Book of Romans. How very valuable to me were the books our faithful and diligent staff leader, Fred Woodberry, gave to me. In between my heavy academic study load, I knew I had to *give time* daily to the Scriptures, and also periodic time to the reading of books by more mature and assured Christians than I. Fred encouraged me to read *Basic Christianity* by John Stott, as well as books with such titles as, *The Fact of Christianity* and *Did Jesus Really Rise from the Dead?* And of course there was always Bill's encouragement. Even though he failed to understand why I had to get so emotional about the whole thing, he continued to give me books by the Danish Christian existentialist, Sören Kierkegaard, and to speak to me of the "leap of faith."

Those months of searching were actually quite bleak to me spiritually. The Scriptures, rather than being inspirational, seemed like sawdust in my mouth. Only because I had made an agreement before God to read the Bible did I continue to do so. I often had to remind myself of what Paul admonished his younger companion Timothy: "Continue thou in the things which thou hast learned and hast been assured of, knowing of whom thou hast learned them; and that from a child thou hast known the holy scriptures, which are able to make thee wise unto salvation through faith which is in Christ Jesus. All scripture is given by inspiration of God, and is profitable for doctrine, for reproof, for correction, for instruction in righteousness: that the man of God may be perfect, throughly furnished unto all good works" (2 Tim. 3:14-17). I was like Timothy, in that early in my life

27

I had learned something of the Bible, but how very much I yet needed to be assured of the validity of its unique claims.

Over the years my tiny bedroom, situated directly between my parents' bedroom on one side and my brother's on the other, had become a spiritual sanctuary or "get-away" place for me. And it was there that I one night began reading the Gospel of John. I audibly read chapter 14, verses 1 through 6. When I got to verse 6, I stopped to ponder the implications of this statement: "Jesus saith unto him, I am the way, the truth, and the life: *no man cometh unto the Father, but by me.*" From this declaration I realized that I wasn't being faced with an optional statement but by an either/or statement. Jesus either *is* the only way—according to His own words—or He is not. If He is not, then He plainly deceived a whole host of people, including myself, and was not worth defending. Soon the issues became even sharper in my mind. I spoke out to a God I was still very unsure of intellectually. "Lord, if You are what this verse says You are, then I'll serve You completely with everything I am and have, but if You are only a figment of someone else's imagination, then I will make my own way in this life, and shape my own values."

One day, while riding a New York City bus, I was reading the Book of First John. At one point in the epistle, the Holy Spirit clearly and unquestionably spoke to my searching heart and mind: "Beloved, believe not every spirit, but try the spirits whether they are of God: because many false prophets are gone out into the world. Hereby know ye the Spirit of God: Every spirit that confesseth that Jesus Christ is come in the flesh is of God" (1 John 4:1-2). The *centrality* and *uniqueness* of *Jesus Christ* as the pivotal issue of life became startlingly clear to me. And a still, small voice spoke plainly to my mind: "My child, if there were any other way for man to be reconciled to Me, I would not have sent My only Son to this world." The chains of oppressive mental doubt finally broke from my mind in the light of the illumination of the Word of God. Jesus Christ divided all of mankind into believers or unbelievers; even history itself was divided from the point of His life and death—B.C., before Christ, or A.D., in the year of our Lord. Each day as people wrote the date of year, they were acknowledging His entrance into recorded history. Clearly, I saw that all truth was to be evaluated and understood from the perspective of the centrality and uniqueness of Jesus Christ. No other prophet or seer claimed such complete victory over death. To the honest inquirer the evidences for His resurrection were irrefutable. Obviously since He was alive, it meant also that all His claims to deity were confirmed by the eternal God! Therefore, when He claimed to be *the* Way, *the* Truth, and *the* Life" that is precisely what He meant; and when He then made the categorical statement, "No man cometh unto the Father, *but by me,"* He meant what He said!

Amazingly, the doubts vanished in the light of the power of His risen life. Jesus was alive, and that fact alone vindicated and made relevant all the words He spoke during His earthly ministry! No longer did I have to *defend* a doctrine or creed, instead I was simply to be a *witness* to the reality of His risen life. Months of intense intellectual confusion finally dissolved at the feet of the risen Lord and Savior.

My remaining years as a philosophy major were filled with the joy of seeing Him vindicate His Truth, and of finding myself becoming more and more secure in the objective reality of the gospel—as well as in the subjective experience of it.

Father, thank You that the "light and darkness" of our personal experiences never changes the fact that You are the objective, eternal Light of the world.

7

The Beginning of a Vision

Where there is no vision, the people perish.
(Prov. 29:18)

And the Lord answered me, and said, Write the vision, and make it plain upon tables, that he may run that readeth it. For the vision is yet for an appointed time, but at the end it shall speak, and not lie: though it tarry, wait for it; because it will surely come, it will not tarry.
(Hab. 2:2-3)

"Do you know that every time you come back to town you start a near riot in the youth group? Do you realize how radical you are in some of your concepts? And does your delivery always have to have 'the hell and brimstone' tone to it? It's great for you to come back home after being gone for months, and give us a fiery sermon or two, but what about those of us who are still here after you're gone? How do we put some of the pieces back together?"

Charlie listened soberly as one sentence after another tumbled out from my agitated spirit. "Never, absolutely never, have I met anyone like you. Some of the kids actually think you're in heresy. And I'm also beginning to wonder. Like, what is this all about anyhow? What's the 'living church' you're talking about? And what do you mean that being a Sunday school teacher is not one of the gifts of the Holy Spirit as listed in Corinthians? And if missionaries aren't present-day apostles, what is an apostle? And if inspired preaching isn't equivalent to the 'prophet' mentioned in Ephesians 4, then what is a prophet? Good nightshirt, Charlie, how can you come home like this and turn our theology all upside down?" By now I knew my face was quite flushed from the fervor of my outburst.

Charlie would come back home from Bible school in Canada only a couple of times a year, but in each instance his coming home was an event. I couldn't deny the fact that it was always challenging to be with him, but it was also a fact that here was someone who just couldn't be content with the status quo of things. And I wasn't sure if this was good or bad. Now here we were sitting on the cement stoop in front of my house discussing his latest revelation on the "living church."

"If you would calm down, and be still for a minute, maybe I could begin answering your questions," Charlie finally interrupted my verbal explosion. I looked at his handsome face, and was once again impressed by the intensity and sincerity which seemed to shine out of his huge brown eyes.

"Look, Dotty, I'm not trying to be radical. It's just that, well, somehow I know there's more to Christianity than what we've experienced so far. There's such a hunger in my heart to know more of the Lord, and more of His power manifested on the earth. While I was in school, the Lord prompted me to get up every morning at four and make an intensive study of Ephesians. The Book has become alive to me. I'm beginning to see the church as He always intended it to be, *alive* with the power of the Holy Spirit. The church is a living organism, not a sterile organization. The head of this church is Jesus himself, and His life is meant to be expressed through every member of His body. The early church didn't meet in big, expensive buildings and with members sitting lifelessly in pews listening to one man do all the preaching and teaching. Dotty, did you ever consider the impact of what Paul said in 1 Cor. 14:26: 'How is it then, brethren? when ye come together, *every one* of you hath a psalm, hath a doctrine, hath a tongue, hath a revelation, hath an interpretation. Let all things be done unto edifying.' "

"Hold on now, Charlie, you're on dangerous doctrinal ground. You know the gifts were only for the early church in its infancy."

"That's just it, Dotty; that infantile church had more of the power of God manifested than we've ever dared to dream about."

"But Charlie, we have the Scriptures; we don't need those gifts anymore. Anyhow, everybody knows that that's just emotionalism."

"I'm not so sure about that anymore, Dotty. I'm beginning to read the Scriptures in a new light. God spoke to me, Dotty, as I was studying Ephesians. He's got something planned for this generation. He's going to do something yet in a practical way to prepare His Bride for His coming. She surely isn't ready to meet Him in the shape she's in now. Dotty, I just know there's more! He's going to move by His Spirit and truly have a visible expression of His mighty life upon the face of the earth. All over the world people will truly praise and worship Him in Spirit and in truth."

"In a minute, you'll be giving an altar call; I can feel it. Oh Charlie, you're so radical! I don't understand everything you're saying! Although something inside of me gets excited about what you're saying, my mind says, 'Watch out!' One important point, though; you don't believe speaking in tongues is for today, do you?"

Charlie's eyes seemed to get even bigger, as a smile cautiously covered his face. "Is there no end to this interrogation?" he jokingly asked.

"Come now, Charlie, don't evade the issue; just what do you think of tongues?"

"You know, while I was counseling at camp in Liberty Corner, New Jersey, last summer, I had an unusual experience. Late one evening as I was walking across the open field under the magnificent beauty of the clear, star-emblazoned summer night, such praise and awe filled my heart for the Lord that I was at a loss to be able adequately to express it. When I got back to my room I said to one of my fellow counselors, 'You know, Wilmer, if ever I could see a reason for speaking in tongues, I sure could see it tonight. Such praise filled my heart for the Lord that my mind could hardly find the words to express it to Him.' So what I'm saying, Dotty, is this: that I'm open to the possibility that all the gifts are for the church today as well as for the first century."

At this point, I heard my mom tap a little impatiently on her bedroom window, which overlooked the front street. Charlie sheepishly grinned, and waved at her. "Boy, Dotty, I'm sorry. It's almost 1:00 A.M. I didn't realize it was getting so late. I'll see ya again sometime before I leave for Canada. Tell your folks I'm sorry I kept you out so long."

As I lay in bed that night, I could hardly sleep. The things about which we spoke ran round and round in my mind. "Oh, Father, could this 'vision' truly be of You? Do You actually have a specific purpose and intent for this generation in which we live?"

Before I could settle down to sleep that night, I just had to look up the verse Charlie said the Lord had given him from Mal. 1:11: "From the rising of the sun even unto the going down of the same my name shall be great among the Gentiles; and in every place incense shall be offered unto my name, and a pure offering: for my name shall be great among the heathen, saith the Lord of hosts."

"In every city, town, village, and hamlet, God will have a free expression of His Body flowing in the power and life of His Spirit," Charlie had emphatically stated. It was now 1958, just a few short years before the groundswell of what would be later known as the charismatic movement.

Needless to say I left our discussion that night with my head reeling, but my heart burning. Some of the concepts and understandings Charlie now held certainly did sound radical, but I could also not deny that what he shared from the New Testament on the church made more scriptural sense to me than anything else I had ever been taught on the Body of Jesus Christ. Charlie left New York for many months, and during that time the spark he had left behind in my heart in regard to the "vision" of a vibrant and alive church was soon to begin burning with an intense fervor within my own soul as well. With new eyes, I began to study the Book of Acts.

Thank you, Father, for the beauty of Your church. Thank You that Your church is made up of living stones, of redeemed people who are learning to reflect Your presence. And thanks too, Father, for those of Your people in whose hearts this vision of a victorious church burns with an increasing fervor.

8

Is That You, Lord?

May he grant you your heart's desire, and fulfil all your plans! May we shout for joy over your victory, and in the name of our God set up our banners! May the Lord fulfil all your petitions!

(Ps. 20:4-5, RSV)

"What does the aesthetic quality of beauty have to do with the gospel anyhow, Al?"

"Dotty, stop being so narrow and opinionated," Al, another college friend of mine, responded after one of our stimulating philosophy courses on aesthetics. And in a few minutes, he and I were once again deeply involved in a very enlivened discussion on the philosophical concept of beauty and form. Walking hurriedly to the Lutheran Student Federation's small campus building to eat our lunch, we soon found ourselves in a rather heated debate with some preseminary students as to whether or not the Bible is the Word of God, or simply *contains* the Word of God. It appeared as though I was always holding the minority opinion.

Truly, I thoroughly enjoyed college! And I thrived in the midst of challenge and debate. Ever since the Lord graciously revealed Jesus' centrality and supremacy in all of life, challenge no longer intimidated me but rather proved to be just the incentive to cause me to seek out more intensely answers from the Scriptures through study and answers from His heart through prayer.

The relationships I had formed in college were very meaningful to me. In fact, life was most exciting. It was just great to be alive and actively learning and growing.

The small Inter-Varsity group that I belonged to was a constant source of strength and refreshment to me. Sometimes only four or five of us would gather to study the Bible and pray during lunch hour. But how alive those studies were. The Gospel of John and the Book of Romans became our main diet. The more we became nvolved in the Scriptures the more of an outlet of witness to others we needed. So every Friday afternoon saw some of us meeting with a number of sociology and anthropology students in the cafeteria to study the claims of Jesus. We challenged them that He could not be accepted simply as a great teacher. According to His own words, He either was God or He was the greatest hoax who ever lived. Thus the cafeteria became an anointed place to present the unique claims of Christ from the Gospel of John.

We also spent much time in prayer, and in intercession for the students on campus. Since so many of them were Jewish, we felt led to hold a series of lectures on the Person of Jesus Christ from the Jewish as well as the Hellenistic point of view.

It was while engaged in the preparation for these meetings that I spent much time in prayer with the little Inter-Varsity group, and also by myself. During the past few months Jesus was completely real in my life. His presence was a constant source of delight to me, and many times while riding the Flushing bus home from college I found myself quietly pouring out my heart to Him.

"I do love You, Lord Jesus. You have become everything to me. I delight in Your ways, and long to know You so much better. You have my life, Lord, for whatever purposes You choose."

It was also during this period that every now and then a thought would pop into my mind. "Lord, You know I'm willing to be single if that's what You want, but don't You think that Ralph's a fine Christian leader? Don't You think we would work out well together?" To this request the Lord specifically spoke to me from Heb. 13:5, "Be content with such things as ye have: for he hath said, I will never leave thee, nor forsake thee."

"But Lord, did You consider. . ."

"Let it suffice thee; speak no more unto me of this matter" (Deut. 3:26). This latter word almost literally leaped from the pages as I was reading. I knew the Lord wanted no more discussion as to whom I thought would be a suitable mate for me.

During these months, a small group of us made a commitment to meet together for prayer every morning before classes began. It soon became evident that the more we got to know the Lord and His ways, the more He was able to share with us His burden for the students on our campus.

One night, during the Christmas recess of 1959, the presence of the Lord was especially real to me. It was already quite late at night, but the gratitude I was feeling toward the Lord for the gift of His Son was overflowing from my heart. Even though the rest of my family were already asleep, I found myself unusually alert and awake. As I was reading through the Psalms, I slipped out of my bed onto my knees.

"Father, use me to make others aware of Your beauty, and of Your glory and love. O, my dear God, cause the eyes of many of the students on our campus to be opened as to who You really are. May the warmth of

Your love pierce through the coldness of hearts, particularly the hearts of the Jewish students, who should especially know that You are the long-awaited Messiah. O God, bring men and women to repentance and faith in You. Lord, what about Eddie? O Jesus, Your hand is upon him, draw him to yourself. And Debbie, thank You that she's acknowledged You as her Messiah. What a change You have made in her life." As I knelt before Him, tears welled up from deep within me. How deeply I felt His longing for those whom He initially called His own. "He came unto his own, and his own received him not," John 1:11 declared. "O Father, pour out Your Spirit upon the natural house of Israel." For the next hour the Lord brought name after name to my mind of those for whom He wanted me to pray.

He had so filled my life that I again told the Lord how happy and content I was to be simply His. In the course of our fellowship, an unusual and unpremeditated statement came out of my mouth. "Lord, if I ever do marry, I have one condition. And that is, that the union of this man and myself will bring more glory to You than what my life would bring You alone!" At that very moment, not only did I experience unspeakable joy and glory in the Father, but I also sensed the joy of His heart in me. That night I *knew* what Peter meant when he wrote: "Whom having not seen, ye love; in whom, though now ye see him not, yet believing, ye rejoice with joy unspeakable and full of glory" (1 Pet. 1:8).

It was during this same time that I began praying for Charlie, and for the actualization of the desire on his heart to see the church restored to vibrancy and power. "Cause that vision for Your church to burn even more deeply upon his soul, Lord. Meet his every need. Release the gifts and ministries within Your church, Lord. O

God, build Your Zion in this hour. . . ." And so the night moved into the early hours of the next morning. At one juncture I simply sat in the holy and restful presence of my Father in absolute silence, and deep in my soul He spoke: "You will one day marry Charles!"

"Lord, was that You? Or was that my imagination? Father, that must have been Your voice!"

I can still remember the excitement which filled my whole being that night. His voice had been unmistakable! My devotional reading had been in the Psalms for the past few weeks, and I was now impressed to continue reading them. On that early winter morning the Lord spoke to me from His Word, as well as by His Spirit within my heart. Psalms 20 and 21 almost leaped from the page in their confirmation of what He had just told me in regard to Charles. Yes, I would one day be Mrs. Charles P. Schmitt, and together we would build in the purposes of God for these last days. How well I remember my closing thoughts before I fell asleep that early morning hour: "O God, that's almost too good to be true!" "Thou hast given [her her] heart's desire, and hast not withheld the request of [her] lips" (Ps. 21:2).

I awoke later that morning and could hardly believe some of the events of the evening before. Somehow things always looked far less spiritual when I would first awake in the morning as the realities of a given day bore down upon me.

"Lord, was that actually You? You know we've never gone out with one another as such. Why, I don't even really know him! And what about love—certainly loving one another is vital to marriage? And what about him, Lord; are You telling *him* the same thing? O Father, I have so many questions!"

But the questions were not to be answered immediately.

I had to simply *trust* Him with my whole life—guidance, questions, and all!

It would take almost four years of dealing, circumstances, and leadings to see the fulfillment of what the Father had spoken to me that early morning hour. Yes, years of learning what David had learned long before: "What man is he that feareth the Lord? him shall he teach in the way that *he* [the Lord] *shall choose*" (Ps. 25:12).

Father, thank You for knowing our every need. And thank You for giving us not what we want but always what we need! And thanks too, Father, that the more we delight in You, we find You give us the desires of our hearts.

9

Living in the Realm of Feeling or Faith?

Thou shalt remember all the way which the Lord thy God led thee these forty years in the wilderness, to humble thee, and to prove thee, to know what was in thine heart, whether thou wouldest keep his commandments, or no.

(Deut. 8:2)

"Surely there will be a letter in the box from him today," I excitedly thought as I almost flew down the block from school on that bleak January afternoon. It had been about three weeks now since that unusually precious night in the presence of the Lord. I certainly expected that if God had spoken to me about Charles He certainly had spoken to Charles about me, unless I had only imagined the whole thing.

And so it had been going for the last couple of weeks. I found myself fluctuating between high experiences of faith and low ones of skepticism and doubt. I finally got to the mailbox. Quickly I flipped through the second-class mail and some bills. "Nothing, nothing, dear God; couldn't he even send a post card indicating that at least he knew I was still alive?" I sighed out loud.

As the weeks passed into months, with still no word from Charles, it became clear to me that I have to shelve the "revelation." It was up to the Lord either to bring it to pass or show me where I had erred. It was not my task to become preoccupied with future events, even if they did have to do with "a word from God." Gently the Father nudged me to deal with present realities. I was to live each day fully to Him and leave the future completely in His capable hands.

My stimulating college career eventually came to an end with my receiving a B.A. in philosophy in June 1960. That summer sovereignly found me counseling in the same Bible camp in New Jersey where Charles had spent so many of his young years. This opportunity had unexpectedly been offered me shortly after graduation from college. It was during my stay at this camp that a teaching position opened up for me in a Christian school in Massachusetts.

That fall, I moved into a large old house located on a hill which overlooked a narrow, winding river. There were eight of us teachers living together, and I was among the youngest. Living in such a community, miles away from home, soon revealed to me just how much I had actually been living in the realm of feeling and in the thrill of an almost pseudo-intellectual academic world of college days.

Suddenly I was faced with the responsibility of teaching the basics of the faith and of life to a lively group of ten-and-eleven-year-olds. (I was actually not too prepared for this task, since my major in college had been philosophy.)

And even back at the teacherage we were constantly discussing how to cook the cheapest yet most nutritious meals rather than the grandiose concepts of Nietzsche or Schopenhauer.

"Now for the fourth time, who has not cleaned up after herself in this bathroom?" Every time Frances asked this question, I couldn't help but feel a little guilty even though there were six of us using the bathroom.

With the increase of practical responsibilities and the decrease of constant outside spiritual and mental stimulation, I came to realize how fragile my practical Christianity in fact was. Learning to live effectively with a group of women who were all so different was a challenge to us all. I experienced seasons of loneliness and discouragement which I had never known before.

"My dear Father, is this what real life is all about for most people? Where is the excitement of running in the purposes of the Lord? O God, I feel so lonely!" To these questions I seemed to get no other answers than those I found in the Gospel accounts: "For which of you, intending to build a tower, sitteth not down first, and counteth the cost, whether he have sufficient to finish it? Lest haply, after he hath laid the foundation, and is not able to finish it, all that behold it begin to mock him, saying, This man began to build, and was not able to finish. . . . So likewise, whosoever he be of you that forsaketh not all he hath, he cannot be my disciple" (Luke 14:28-30, 33). My heavenly Father was speaking a clear word to me. "You have learned enough of the *theory* of My ways; now put it into practice both when you feel like it and when you *don't.*" Living in community with other people quickly allows us to see how much of His life is merely spoken about, and how much has actually been appropriated. Truly these were days of growing up.

Someone has aptly defined maturity as the ability of postponing an immediate pleasure for the attainment of a long-range goal. As I learned how to maintain a job responsibly on a daily basis and how to live selflessly with other people, my lack of emotional maturity surprised me. God may have spoken a glorious word as to what my future would be, but presently He was interested in causing His daughter to mature spiritually and emotionally in very practical, humdrum, everyday situations.

These first few years after college were times of proving and testing the commitment of my heart. For so long I had asked, "Lord, help me to trust *You*." It now appeared as though He were saying, "Daughter, can I trust *you*? Will you stand under pressure? Will you believe even in the darkness of circumstances? Will you give to others even when you feel you have need of being given to? Will you trust Me in the humdrum of the everyday?"

"Whosoever will come after me, let him deny himself, and take up his cross, and follow me. . . . And whosoever of you will be the chiefest, shall be servant of all" (Mark 8:34; 10:44). And Charles? Well, that was a whole other area of my life.

Father, You're so practical! Thank You for the mountain-peak experiences, and thank You for being in the valley with us. But probably the best thing is that You walk with us in our everyday lives, when the only special thing about the day is that we know You as Father.

10

So, What If I'm Wrong?

He shall not be afraid of evil tidings: his heart is fixed, trusting in the Lord. His heart is established, he shall not be afraid.

(Ps. 112:7-8)

From the time the Lord spoke to me of Charles on that early winter morning in late December 1959 to my graduation from college in June 1960, I received about three epistles from Charles. And epistles they were! One was on the significance of scriptural water baptism, about which he was writing a pamphlet. Another was on the difference between the "church" and the "work" according to Watchman Nee*, and the third had something to do with Paul's understanding of "head coverings." I just could not believe the nature of his letters! "Dear God, I do enjoy all of this theology, but what about a personal word from him to me. Are You saying anything to him about our relationship?"

Again and again the Lord indicated that I was not to become distracted by anything but to live my life to the

---

*An outstanding influential servant of the Lord in China during the twentieth century whose recorded spoken ministry has in recent decades been translated and published in English. Because of his faith he suffered twenty years imprisonment in Communist China and died in 1972.

fullest in this present hour. Concerning my questions about Charles, only one word was quickened to me: "Sit still, My daughter, until thou know how the matter will fall: for the man will not be in rest, until he have finished the thing this day" (Ruth 3:18). (I was to learn that a "day" for the Lord may be quite a length of time for *us!*)

"Great, Lord! Rest! Rest? How does a person rest when the course of one's entire life seems to be at stake?"

To these impassioned cries of my heart the Lord simply said, "Rest, My daughter, comes from getting to know Me better. Have you grasped the significance of the fact that I am the Creator of heaven and earth, that all power, and authority, and dominion are Mine? Do you know that I am the Alpha and the Omega, the beginning and the end of all things? Have you considered the fact that I who once was dead am alive forevermore?"

To these stirrings within my heart was added the passage from Jer. 32:27: "Behold, I am the Lord, the God of all flesh: is there any thing too hard for me?" Increasingly I began to realize that rest cannot be conjured up by trying harder to do something. His rest comes as a result of a growing revelation and illumination as to who He actually is. No wonder Jesus so emphasized the necessity of coming to Him: "Come unto me, all ye that labour and are heavy laden, and I will give you rest. Take my yoke upon you, and learn of me; for I am meek and lowly in heart: and ye shall find rest unto your souls. For my yoke is easy, and my burden is light" (Matt. 11:28-30).

The grace to release the whole situation of Charles to the Lord worked until the Christmas recess. I returned home for two weeks from my teaching position in Massachusetts. Charles also returned home for a visit from Minnesota, where he had been laboring in the ministry with another young man, Morrie Watson, whom he had met in Bible school.

"Hello, Dotty. Well, Morrie and I are back in town again for a short period of time. Maybe we could get together sometime," Charles' melodious voice rang through the phone.

"I'd love that," I responded. "Maybe Gisela, Carolyn, and Eugene could join us. We could all get together here some evening."

As I waited for them all to come, I was getting more and more nervous. I brushed my hair numerous times. I chuckled to myself, wondering if I were subconsciously trying to make it longer, since I knew Charles liked long hair. I dabbed at my lipstick countless times so it wouldn't be too dark, because he didn't like makeup either—he thought it was too worldly.

The bell rang! Before I could even unlock the door I heard the quick steps of long legs on the staircase, and I knew Charles and Morrie had arrived.

The evening was profitably spent discussing the "end-time purposes of God." I couldn't help but wonder what this vibrant young man was really like. It sure would be good to know something of the man himself, if I were indeed going to marry him. But this possibility of marriage looked even more remote to me at the conclusion of our time together.

"You know, Dorothy, the Lord is speaking to some of us about the implications of 1 Corinthians 7 for our lives today. I'm seriously considering the possibility that the Lord may want me to remain unmarried so I can serve Him without distraction."

As Charles was honestly sharing his heart, I could feel my face turning crimson. I knew that the expression on my face defied description. After a moment of awkward

silence, I took a deep breath and said, "Oh, how nice."
Immediately I realized how stupid that must have
sounded, and quickly attempted to respond with a more
spiritual statement.

"Yes, God is certainly looking for such radical commitment during these days." I was hoping this response
didn't sound as hollow to him in the hearing of it as it did
to me in the speaking of it. Finally everyone left, and I
literally ran to my little bedroom.

Had I been completely deceived? Had this all been the
deception of my own mind and heart? How could God
have spoken one word to me, and such a seemingly
different word to him? Doubts began to fill my mind as
the tears crowded my eyes.

"God, where *are* You in all of this?" As I sat on my bed, I
said out loud: "Lord, if You've allowed me to be deceived in
this matter, and if I've been so wrong, how can I ever trust
You again? If this has all been a conjecture of my own
imagination then I'll, I'll. . ." Immediately a section of
Scripture came to me from John: "Then said Jesus unto the
twelve, Will ye also go away? Then Simon Peter answered
him, Lord, to whom shall we go? thou hast the words of
eternal life. And we believe and are *sure* that thou art that
Christ, the Son of the living God" (John 6:67-69). I just sat
there, allowing these words to sink into my bewildered
mind and heart. Finally it dawned on me: *Where* was I to go?
Who else had the words of eternal life? "Well, Lord, I guess
we're stuck with one another. If I am wrong, then we'll
start all over again. But You have become my very life, and
there is no other One to whom I can go."

Peace filled my heart and mind. I didn't have any more
answers, but I had Him! Once again, I was experiencing
the warmth of His love that had years before begun its
work within my life. No, even if I had misinterpreted and

49

misunderstood His leadings, I could go to no one else! For it was His love and His faithfulness that was the basis of my life!

Charles and I spent a few more "theologically" lively hours together, at the conclusion of which he returned to Minnesota, and I, to Massachusetts. The days and months which were to follow would find me digesting more and more of the truths of the Bible, and drawing more and more strength from Him in order to live my life daily for Him and for others.

Thank You, Father, that Your mature love heals the immaturity of our feelings of fear and insecurity. Thank You for establishing us in this love, and for patiently leading us in Your perfect ways as well as in Your exact timing.

11

Freedom of Truth,
or Ensnarement of Deception?

*My sheep hear my voice, and I know them, and
they follow me: and I give unto them eternal
life; and they shall never perish, neither shall
any man pluck them out of my hand.*

(John 10:27-28)

"Dorothy, you have leadership qualities, and have
much zeal, and that is why some of us on staff have a
concern for you," Dr. Garbe, my faculty advisor from
seminary, gently admonished me.

The past two years had been profitably spent teaching
elementary levels in Christian schools. Since graduation
from college there had been a growing hunger in my
heart to receive further training, especially in the area
of the Scriptures. In the spring of 1962 the Lord began
impressing upon me to move in this direction. And thus
that fall I began my studies at Biblical Seminary in New
York City.

All during this time I received letters from Charles
encouraging me to be open to the "new, glorious, end-
time move of God" which was beginning to touch various
denominational people.

While in seminary, the Lord brought together a group
of people who were hungry for more of the Lord. What a
challenging time for us! Frequently a number of us met
for prayer and for further study of the Bible. We began

looking into the gifts and ministries of the Holy Spirit. Then, during March 1963, God moved significantly within the lives of many of the students, for with each passing day there was yet another student who experienced more of what Jesus meant when He said, "I am come that they might have life, and that they might have it more abundantly" (John 10:10).

The Lord had sovereignly brought to the seminary that year a young woman who had been a missionary overseas. While she was in India, the Lord had baptized Flossie in the Holy Spirit and had given her the gift of prophecy. With great wisdom Flossie allowed the Lord to use her in very natural and "unreligious" ways. When she shared a prophetic word with us, she neither changed her tone of voice nor became shaky in her physical gestures (which phenomena I had skeptically observed taking place in some pentecostal circles in previous days), but instead spoke to us in a quite natural, conversational manner.

During one of our prayer times together in seminary, the Lord spoke to us by a prophetic word. I was stunned—because it came out of my own mouth! It was about the first time I had even consciously recognized the prophetic gift at work within me. As a result of our study on the gifts of the Spirit a number of us had decided we knew how God would distribute them. First He would give the gift of tongues, and then the other gifts would follow. It was in the midst of some of these conclusions that the Lord himself prophetically spoke to us: "You cannot box Me in, My children. I am far greater than any of your theological conclusions and deductions. I am the God of all flesh. Why do you limit the Holy One of Israel, even as My people of old did? Watch, I will now surprise you as to how I will work in your lives."

And surprise it was! During the month of March a number of students experienced for themselves the different gifts of the Spirit. One young man found his mouth filled with words he had never before learned, and this occurred to him while sitting in a homiletics class! (He afterward shared that he could hardly wait for the class to end so that he could get to his own room and allow the words to be given audible expression.) Another, a young woman, always responded when someone was sick. She began experiencing different gifts of healing flowing through her when difficult situations would arise in other people's lives. Thus it soon became obvious that the gift of faith was uniquely operative within her. And I myself came into a greater awareness of the gift of prophecy working through me.

Now it was at this time, as was mentioned earlier, that I was asked to come and receive counsel from my faculty advisor. As I was sharing these things with Dr. Garbe, she wisely cautioned me, "You know, Dorothy, even from your limited knowledge of church history, that many cults and sects have been spawned by women of strong personalities who came under serious deception."

These words rang through my mind during the next few days. I found a growing alarm arising in my heart. "O dear God, here I am again! Am I hearing *Your* voice? Is this truly a move of *Your* Spirit, or am I being deluded and deceived? Is the church truly being revived and restored, or is this simply a trick to lead Your people more deeply into the muck and mire of confusion and division? O Lord, why does it seem to be so hard to clearly discern Your voice at times?"

To add to my dilemma, I had been receiving a few more letters from Charles. He was sharing how God was beginning to pour out His Spirit upon more and more denominational people. It was true! Even at seminary we were hearing about Episcopalians, Lutherans, and Presbyterians being "baptized in the Holy Spirit.""This is but the beginning of a real outpouring of His Spirit to restore the church to the New Testament pattern,"Charles would write. But how did I know for sure this was true, especially when people whom I deeply respected were warning me of error and deception? Once again I could only turn to the Scriptures for light and instruction. With renewed fervor I began reading the Bible for some more answers.

Since I commuted to seminary by subway, I used this time to read the Book of John. (I'm sure that angels have smiled at times over the unlikely places God's people have found for studying the Holy Scriptures. The New York subways, crowded and filled to capacity with every size, shape, color, and disposition of person, makes it a unique "quiet place.") It was during one of these challenging subway rush hours that the Lord spoke to me from John 10. Even though the car was quite crowded, it was as though the Lord and I were alone. Together we feasted on the truths of the Good Shepherd and His dealings with His sheep. The dialogue went something like this:

"My child, how have I uniquely revealed Myself to you?"

"Why Lord, from my earliest experiences of You, it was as if I most intimately knew You as my Good Shepherd. You know, Lord, how impressed I always was with that multicolored stained-glass window-picture of You as a shepherd carrying a sheep in Your arms."

"If I am your Shepherd, then what does that make you?"

"Well then, I am Your sheep; and as such, Lord, You

know I'm pretty dumb at times."

"If you therefore as My sheep get into the wrong pasture, whose responsibility is it to get you back into the right one?"

I sat there in amazement in the midst of all the bustle of the morning rush hour. I was experiencing a deep sense of joy and release.

"Why, Lord, if I get into the wrong pasture, You as my Good Shepherd, with Your rod and staff, are responsible to get me back into the right pasture."

"And how many times have I not already rescued you from the bramble bushes, and guided you away from parched pastures? Can you not also trust Me now?"

How can one adequately express the joy of having heard the voice of the Good Shepherd! It seemed like the chains of fear and anxiety literally fell from me to the floor of that subway car. He knew I loved Him. He also knew *I wanted to be corrected* if I were in error. And hence, I was His responsibility! As long as I walked in the light I had, and kept an open heart before Him and His people, it was His responsibility to lead me into the right pastures. What a relief to belong to the Great Shepherd of the sheep!

That precious experience on the subway—and the revelation of His shepherding heart—was to be my confidence and foundation in many other future circumstances. Once more another of the Lord's sheep had learned by experience the truth which has sounded forth throughout many ages: "The Lord is my shepherd; I shall not want. He maketh me to lie down in green pastures: he leadeth me beside the still waters. He restoreth my soul: he leadeth me in the paths of righteousness for *his name's sake*" (Ps. 23:1-3).

Father, can we ever adequately express the joy we have in truly getting to know You? What a freedom we come into as we realize You are protecting us from false voices and leading us into green pastures, and that You as our heavenly Father are also our Good Shepherd. Thank You for Your rod and Your staff, which You use both to correct us and to protect us.

12

Through It All

Thou wilt keep him in perfect peace, whose mind is stayed on thee: because he trusteth in thee.

(Isa. 26:3)

It was a distinctly cold December morning. If it hadn't been for all the people jammed into the Lexington Avenue. subway, I know even the subways would have been uncomfortably cold. I hurriedly climbed the subway steps at the East 49th Street exit. Glancing at the clock, I knew I'd barely make it to the Monday morning prayer meeting at seminary.

"Dear Lord, I sure don't mean to be a pest, but right now I need some objective input into my life in regard to Charles. Your Word seemed again to be so clear to me last night, but I know how deceptive the heart and emotions can be. O Lord, I'm looking to You," I prayed as I partially ran, partially walked, through the cold and busy streets on New York's east side.

The events of the preceding night were very fresh in my mind. I had just received word that morning from Charles' mom that he would soon be back in town.

"Great, Lord, I'm so glad I do hear from him," was my first disappointed reaction to his mom's announcement. For the remainder of the day I had found myself wondering what this visit would bring forth. I was especially nervous since I knew he had been made aware of my "revelation" from a concerned mutual friend. "O dear God, how humiliating! Why don't we just forget the whole thing, Lord. It sure would seem easier right now than to have to face him, and explain my revelation. Anyhow, Lord, it's not *my* revelation, it's *Yours,* so *You* handle this whole thing!" I both prayed and groaned for most of the afternoon.

Towards evening I finally quieted myself sufficiently to be able to make some sense out of the assignments from seminary. I was taking a course in Luke and in Acts. I was presently studying the Book of Luke. As I was rereading the first chapter, my eyes became fixed upon verse 45: "Blessed is she that believed: for there shall be a performance of those things which were told her from the Lord." The words stood out from the page and burned themselves into my heart. "No, My daughter, you have not been deceived; trust Me, it shall surely come to pass," came the quiet assurance of my Shepherd's voice to my heart.

It was good to come into the warmth of the seminary entryway. Even running from the subway these three blocks didn't seem to make me any warmer. I quickly hung up my coat and quietly slipped into the back of the comfortable first-floor lounge where some of the students were gathered to pray. I didn't exactly know why, but I just wanted to cry. "O Lord, why do I want to cry? This is no way to start a new week." It was no use. I just sat in the back of the room and cried as those around me enthusiastically prayed and sang.

As the prayer meeting was being concluded, Flossie walked towards me. "Say, Dot, I really feel I am to pray with you. Why don't you come with me to one of the side rooms?" As I knelt down in the small room, Flossie put her hand upon my head and began to pray. After a few minutes she began praying in another tongue. At the conclusion of the tongue there was a brief pause, after which she gave the interpretation: "Blessed is she that believed: for there shall be a performance of those things which were told her from the Lord."

With eyes wide as saucers, I stared at her in stunned silence. Simultaneously laughing and crying, I tried to ask an intelligible question. "How, how, I mean when, or rather who . . . ? Oh, Flossie, how did you know what that tongue meant, and did you know that last night—oh, no, you couldn't have known. O Lord, thank You!" Now I really cried, but from gratitude to the Lord. Not only did He reassure me that I had indeed heard Him speak, but He also confirmed the fact that the gifts were for this hour as well as for the first-century church.

The days couldn't pass quickly enough for Charles to return home from Minnesota. Certainly the Lord had now finally spoken to him as well. With mixed emotions I found myself jumping every time the phone rang on the day he was to return to New York. At last towards evening, the long awaited call came. "Praise the Lord, Dotty, Morrie and I finally made it home. Just wanted to check in with you and find out how things were doing. Tomorrow is pretty much tied up, but maybe I can come over the next day sometime." And so Charles was home, as impersonal as ever; but at least he was home.

Friday eventually arrived. Charles thought it would be a good idea for us to take a drive. We talked about school, Minnesota, scriptural water baptism, and the breaking of bread. Then, about a block from my home, Charles pulled to the curb. "Well, Dotty, I believe there is something we need to discuss." I was amazed as to the complete rest I was experiencing as I heard him say,

"Would you like to tell me about the word from the Lord you feel you received about us?"

"This was not how I had imagined this to work, Lord; *You're* supposed to tell him, not me" was my silent response. Taking a deep breath, I looked out the car window, intently staring up at the cold, star-filled night.

"Boy, Charles, this is a little strange, but here goes." I then proceeded to tell him all the pertinent events leading to this present evening.

When I finished, Charles rolled down his window, leaned his head out, took a deep breath, looked up to the Lord, and said, "Well, Lord, what do You have to say about all of this?" He then gave me a long look and said, "You know that some of us are considering remaining single, Dotty. So far, that doesn't seem to have changed." I gulped, and yet at the same time I felt more at peace about the whole thing than I could ever remember having felt.

When I finally got back into my little room my heart was strangely at peace and in perfect rest. That night before retiring, the Lord quickened to me all of 2 Chronicles 20, especially verse 17: "Ye shall not need to fight in this battle: set yourselves, stand ye still, and see the salvation of the Lord with you."

"Yes, Lord, my life is Yours; I only want Your will, and I praise You; yes, I really praise You."

Charles left New York. I did receive a few more letters than usual, but all of them were impersonal, beginning with "Dear sister Dorothy," and ending with "Yours in Him, brother Charles." But praise the Lord, my mind was stayed upon Him and my hands were full of meaningful activity. The future was in His hands, and meanwhile the present was to be lived and enjoyed for His glory!

Thanks, Lord, it's great to walk with You: and even when our minds don't understand all that's happening, we can praise You with our whole heart.

13

He Leadeth Me in Green Pastures

Shew me thy ways, O Lord; teach me thy paths.
Lead me in thy truth, and teach me: for thou art
the God of my salvation; on thee do I wait all
the day.

(Ps. 25:4-5)

The gray, cold winter months soon turned into brisk New York City March winds, and then finally the warmth of springtime was felt everywhere. Our lunch hours at school during those balmy days were often spent walking through the unusual east-side streets of art galleries, antique shops, and foreign restaurants. Little did I then know that the dawning of this new season of the year was also to be the dawning of a totally new day in my life!

School was fast approaching its conclusion. It had been a stimulating year of study, learning, and growth in the ways of my God. The fellowship among the students had been exceedingly rich and rewarding. Praise God, it was so good to be alive in this hour to serve the Lord!

Towards the middle of May, Charles and Morrie again made their appearance in New York. On a number of occasions, Charles accompanied me to school. "We are living in an hour in which God is beginning to pour out His Spirit all over the earth. These are the end times, and require an absolutely radical commitment to Him and to

His purposes. This is not the time to consider our own comforts, and our own security; it is the time to rebuild the house of the Lord. The prophet Haggai, in chapter 1, verses 4 and 8, strongly exhorted the people: 'Is it time for you, O ye, to dwell in your [paneled] houses, and this house lie waste? . . . Go up to the mountain, and bring wood, and build the house; and I will take pleasure in it, and I will be glorified, saith the Lord.' "

As I heard Charles share his heart and vision for the church with a number of students, I was amazed how very much I felt linked with him in purpose and goal. As he continued sharing the Scriptures, I admiringly observed him. He sat on the edge of the large brown lounge chair, his long arms and expressive hands moving continously as he spoke. A lock of his dark, well-groomed hair fell over his finely chiseled brow, and his large brown eyes flashed fervently as with great intensity he continued to speak of the house God wanted in this hour. "My dear God, I do love this man," I found myself thinking.

Most of May we spent together visiting small fellow-ships and groups of people in the area. More and more I was being knit with this man. Yet nothing had changed in our relationship. We were simply good friends, who more and more shared the same vision!

"Say, Dotty, why don't you consider coming with us to Minnesota this summer?" Charles asked one afternoon as we were returning home from visiting some people. "We're going to have some tent meetings in Deer River, and we could sure use some help with the women and children. What do you think?"

"Well, I don't know," I responded, a little surprised at his question. "I really don't think my folks would be too enthusiastic. Since I have one more year of seminary left, they sort of expect me to work this summer." In the back of my mind I was also thinking of a number of close friends who were returning home to the city from college for the summer, and whom I wanted to see. "Well, I'll pray about it anyhow," I concluded, as I climbed out of the car and headed up the stairs to our small apartment.

A growing anticipation began filling my heart. "Lord, would You perhaps want me to spend the summer in Minnesota? I have enough finances from teaching to cover my last year at seminary. But my folks, O dear Lord, my folks—whatever will they say?" As I rambled on before the Lord, I seemed to gain increasing peace within about this possibility of going to the upper Midwest for the summer. "Lord, if this is really of You, I trust You to give my parents rest about it. Also, Lord, I'm looking to the Scriptures for a word of confirmation."

My parents had not always understood some of the decisions and religious inclinations of their beloved daughter. But they had always provided a solid and happily secure family environment for my brother and myself to grow up in. My dad especially knew that I deeply respected his counsel and advice, and I had early learned that without his OK it just wasn't to be done.

"Well, Mama, what do you think?"

"I don't know, Dotty. Don't you believe you should begin thinking about settling down a little bit? You know that you'll soon be twenty-five. You can't spend your whole life jumping from place to place."

"I know, Mom. But I really believe the Lord is in this."

My dad frowned. "The Lord this, and the Lord that. Dotty, someday you're going to learn that you can't expect the Lord to do everything for you."

"But, Daddy, He won't take care of me any less than you do. You know He's my heavenly Father."

"Albert, I don't know if it's good for her to spend so much time with that Charlie. I think he's a fanatic."

"Ya, well, if that's going to make her happy. . . . Maybe if she sees how poor they live out there, she'll come to her senses." And so our discussion went that evening. My parents were just slightly open to the possibility of my going to Minnesota for the summer (which to me was in itself a miracle!).

The next morning, as I was seeking the Lord in prayer and in the Scriptures, my devotional reading took me to the Book of Micah. While reading the second chapter, the first part of verse 10 arrested my attention: "Arise ye, and depart; for this is not your rest." During the next couple of days this verse surfaced in my reading on three different occasions. After further discussion with my parents, and with Charles, I concluded that the Lord was indeed saying that I was to "arise and depart" to the northlands of Minnesota.

On May 31, 1963, my father helped pile me into the already overcrowded Volkswagen with the words, "Now watch out, drive carefully, and take good care of my daughter." And so Charles, Morrie, and I pulled away from the curb in front of my house on Gates Avenue to begin our three-day trek west. We were to stop at the homes of different believers on the way out. Once in Minnesota, I was to stay in the home of a Christian family who was part of the small fellowship Charles and Morrie had begun.

So with songs, praises, and much enthusiastic discussion and laughter, we traveled on a journey which would forever determine the course of my life.

Father, I love You! Thank You, thank You,

for guiding Your people. Thank You that You cause goodness and mercy to follow us all the days of our life. Thank You that we can greatly rejoice in Your purpose for our lives.

14

The Beginning of a New Day

This is the day which the Lord hath made; we will rejoice and be glad in it.

(Ps. 118:24)

"Charles, why do you wear mostly browns and blacks? And don't you and Morrie own any ties?" I asked one Sunday afternoon, after I embarrassingly realized that Charles and Morrie were the only ones not to have ties on when we visited with a denominational group of people who were open to the things of the Spirit.

"Well, Dotty, it's worldly. And the Lord is dealing with us on worldliness."

"Is that why you use salt rather than toothpaste, and old Sears catalogues rather than toilet paper?" I asked, partially amused and partially alarmed.

"Well, no, we use those things because we can't afford to buy the real stuff."

How vividly I remember my arrival in northern Minnesota. I stepped into the three-room house which Charles and Morrie and some other young men had rented when they first arrived in Deer River. In the sink was a bucket of water rather than faucets, and the linoleum was clean but worn thin from use. An old potbellied stove stood in the middle of the living room.

"You know, when it gets really cold here, we use newspapers to layer our blankets with. It works great," Morrie enthusiastically informed me.

"But what about a bathroom?" I hesitantly asked.

"Well, we have a great outhouse," said Charles, "only you can't stay in it too long when it gets to be twenty or thirty degrees below zero. And then we have a large tub which we periodically pull into the kitchen and fill up for baths." Charles was trying to be very serious, but a restrained smile finally broke into an uproarious laugh as he watched the bewildered expression on my face.

"Oh, come on now, you've got to lose some of your sophisticated New York City ways and become a little more rugged, and less worldly," Charles continued. "How do you think the pioneers lived?"

"Are you willing to live this way, My daughter?" a still small voice seemed to be nudging me from within.

"No, no Lord! What would my family think? Lord, I have a degree in philosophy, and seminary training; why would You want to put me way out here in this no-man's land? I'm more comfortable with college students, and not with young people, some of whom can't even read. Lord, do You know what You're doing in my life? Anyhow, Charles hasn't even suggested the possibility of marriage; and though I may have his vision for the church, I sure don't agree with him on what worldliness is. Oh, dear Lord, help me!"

I walked, talked, argued, and cried before the Lord for a good while that bright sunny June afternoon. Soon the wind picked up and began blowing gently against my face. "Be still, and know that I am God: I will be exalted among the heathen, I will be exalted in the earth" flashed refreshingly across my mind (Ps. 46:10). I stopped my pacing back and forth in the field, and looked intently at some of the wild flowers blowing in the breeze. At last I looked up into the virtually cloudless sky. I sighed from deep within: "Yes, Lord, You are Lord, and I'm willing to be what You want me to be, go where You want me to go, and live as You want me to live." I then lifted my hands upward to the God who had promised never to leave me nor forsake me.

"Do you know how to use a pressure cooker?" Charles asked, as I was trying to figure out what porcupine meatballs were.

"Well, no, I don't, but I do know how to cook."

"Well, porcupine meatballs need to be made in a pressure cooker, especially because it's so late. What were you doing out in the back field so long anyhow?"

"Oh, just having a session with the Lord."

"Say, can you plant a garden, and can vegetables, and make fruit preserves?"

"Well, no, not really. You know I was brought up in the city, but those are things anyone can learn."

"So you studied philosophy, but you can't can tomatoes and pickles. You know, those are pretty important things around here. How about baking bread?"

"Well, no, I haven't done that either, but I sure do love to cook," I answered enthusiastically, somehow hoping to make up for my other glaring defects.

Charles took me with him as he visited different people in the area. He seemed more quiet than usual, and frequently I'd look up from what I was doing only to find him intently observing me. He would allow me to answer the questions when people asked who we were and what we believed. One evening, as we sat with a few other folks, he intently looked at me and asked, "Dotty, how would you respond if you ever married a man who felt God calling him to be away from home for a month or two at a time, in the work of the gospel?"

I gulped, "Well, I don't know. I guess I had not really ever considered that possibility."

"A lot of women, you know, are clinging-vine types. They have no real walk with the Lord, and no vision for His church, and often drain all the life out of their husbands. Now these end times call for a radical commitment from both men and women. Is the kingdom of God really first in your life?" There was his fanatical zeal again! It both alarmed me and also so very much drew me to him.

"Charles, I simply believe that God will not lead me where His grace cannot keep me."

"Hm, well, I just know that this generation will require our 'utmost for His highest'," Charles concluded our conversation, quoting as he did from Oswald Chambers.

"Gisela, it's like he's putting me into test situations. I just don't understand him. He seems to be very cautious about our relationship."

"Dotty, just be patient. The Lord has it all under His control," she calmly responded to my bewildered questionings. Gisela, by now a very close friend of mine, had decided to spend the two weeks of her vacation from her New York job visiting us in Minnesota and helping us in the children's work. It was so good to be with her. A family allowed us both to stay in a small trailer in front of their house. It was encouraging to have her to pray and share with.

"Say, Gisela, Morrie sure seems to enjoy giving you studies from the Scriptures," I amusingly commented, after she'd been with us for almost a week. Her face flushed a little crimson.

"Dotty, I do believe that he's God's choice for me."

"Wouldn't that be a riot, Gisela! Can you imagine us two New York City sophisticates out here in the northlands of Minnesota with the bears, wild rice, and huge mosquitoes? And *you* can't can tomatoes either!" We both literally rolled on the little couch doubled up with laughter until the tears ran down our cheeks. I was only trusting that the Lord was laughing too!

"Tell me, Dotty, why do you want to marry me?" Charles' question stunned me. We were driving over to a young woman's house to counsel with her, and Charles had asked if I would accompany him. His question was totally unrelated to anything we had been talking about.

Taken by complete surprise, I found myself looking into his large, inquiring brown eyes, and answering, "Because I love you." His eyes became big as saucers, and I thought for sure he would drive the little VW right up the telephone pole. "Charles, honestly, I know we have the same vision and all, but really, is it so shocking that I should also be in love with you?"

He just looked at me a few moments, smiled, and then began humming, "The Church's one foundation is Jesus Christ her Lord."

I could not believe this unusual response. "Lord," I silently cried out, "this is not the time to sing a hymn!"

In less than five minutes we were driving into the yard of the woman's house with whom we had the appointment. During the two hours we were with her Charles said virtually nothing. He merely kept looking at me.

As soon as we got back into the little brown VW, he looked directly at me and said, "Tell me again how you love me differently from the way you would love brother Morrie."

"Oh, Charles, you are so funny! It's not Morrie the Lord said I would marry, it's you. And anyhow, I think the Lord has some other plans for Morrie."

"Yeah, so I noticed. He and Gisela seem to be having a lot of spiritual fellowship lately." We both laughed rather nervously!

Charles spent the next few days much alone, often taking long walks through the woods. Little did I know then that he was very much taking to heart a prophecy spoken over him in California a number of years before, in which he was warned to be very cautious as to his choice of mate. There was one, said this personal prophecy, who would be as a chain around his ankle. And thus he was to be careful, and wait for the Lord to bring the one of His choice to him. So, unbeknown to me, Charles was waiting on the Lord to know whether I was the chain or the choice.

On the Fourth of July a whole group of us went to Thief River Falls for a day of fellowship with some of the believers there. On the way to Thief River, we stopped in a little town for something cold to drink. It was hot, but as usual a refreshing breeze was blowing through the trees from the lake which was at the edge of the little town.

"Dotty, I'm mailing this letter to your parents today. In it, I'm asking your father's permission to marry you. We'll get formally engaged in August and married in December."

I stopped in the middle of the street, startled by his decisive words. With my heart beating quite fast, it suddenly dawned on me that this man, about whom the Lord had spoken to me four years prior, had just *told* me I was going to marry him in December!

72

On December 21, 1963, I became Mrs. Charles P. Schmitt! And the passage of Scripture which had spoken much to me at different times during the past four years became real in my own experience also: "And Isaac . . . took Rebekah, and she became his wife; and he loved her" (Gen. 24:67).

Father, thank You that You make and order the days of our life. And thanks also that with great patience and totally accurate precision You know when best to fulfill Your promises to us. Father, we rejoice in Your choice for us.

15

Adapt or Resist?

*And I will give them one heart, and one way,
that they may fear me for ever, for the good of
them, and of their children after them.*

(Jer. 32:39)

"How come if I love him so much, I still find it so hard
to submit to him as my husband? It just doesn't seem fair
that *I* always have to give in. Anyhow, he's such a perfec-
tionist! I doubt if I'll ever learn to please him," I sobbed
before the Lord. At the time, I was in our little red and
white bedroom located in the back of our recently purchased ten-by-fifty-five-foot cozy green and white mobile home. It was situated on a lovely wooded lot overlooking the Mississippi River. Only a few yards to our
left sat Morrie and Gisela's little mobile home. (Yes, they
too had married—and only two weeks prior to Charles
and myself.) It was a delightful setting, and the love that
filled my heart for Charles was unrivaled by anything I
had previously experienced for anyone. I knew without
the slightest doubt that I was in God's perfect will for my
life, but somehow the adjustments to married life still
were more than I had expected.

"Have you set up the women's Bible study in Deer
River yet? And did you return those phone calls to the
two gals who were having some problems?" Charles had

asked the afternoon before as he returned home from some pastoral calls and from having just completed his Raleigh and Watkins route. (The Lord had opened the door for both him and Morrie to do some part-time selling.)

His eyes showed his disappointment as I responded, "Well, no, I was trying to bake that wheat bread, and ran into a few snares."

"Did you follow the recipe *exactly*?"

"Well, sort of."

"Dotty, when you are just learning to bake you can't be creative." His voice trailed off as he walked back into our little bedroom.

"Well," I angrily thought to myself, "you'd think he'd at least be glad I'm trying!" How totally unreasonable and unfair he was at times.

"Say, where are my brown socks? Oh, no, don't tell me the tan shirt is still unironed! Honestly, Dotty, what did you do all day?" Charles hotly asked from the back room. Tears began filling my eyes.

"You didn't even see the fact that the floors are all waxed, and I also cleaned the stove and refrigerator, as well as baked the bread. Nothing I ever do seems to be enough for you." My voice now audibly quivered as the tears began to flow freely.

Charles walked exasperatedly into the little blue and white kitchen—which was located at the front of the home—and put his long arms around me. "My dear, please don't cry again; you know I'm used to running a tight ship, and when I say I want something done I don't want to wait a week for it to be done."

"Well, I'm trying. But it's never good enough for you. I seem to be a constant disappointment to you." I wept even harder, and pushed myself out of his arms and ran to the little bathroom where I locked myself in. "Boy, what happened to the glamour of it all? Where is God in all of this?" I sobbed to myself as I dejectedly sat on the rim of the bathtub. Needless to say, supper was eaten in somewhat of a strained atmosphere that night.

I was also a little homesick for city life, and especially for my family back in New York. "Lord, do You know what You're doing with us? You haven't forgotten us, have You?" I asked one morning as I put my head against the big window overlooking the partially frozen river. We had gotten another couple of inches of snow the day before, and now the temperature was again dropping below zero. I hadn't realized it could actually get so cold. "Is this really where You want us, away from everything familiar to me?" Lately when I talked to the Lord it was but a monologue. My prayers appeared to go no higher than the ceiling of our little home. Even the Word, which had always been a delight to study, had become dry and dull to me lately. After a while I stared blankly out of the window, feeling almost as cold on the inside as the ice and snow must have been on the outside. As I was reflecting on how very quiet everything was, I remembered all the clothes lying on our bed. Charles wanted me to sort my dresses and suits, as well as my shoes.

"Some of your clothes are just too sophisticated for out here; and how can you walk in those high heels? I told you before that I want my wife to look more homey. I want you to get some nice flowered house dresses rather than those tailored suits."

And so we had had another go-around the night before. I had already removed my lipstick because he didn't want me looking worldly. My hair was longer than it had ever been, in order to please him. "Lord, does submission mean that I simply become a mindless dishrag? Am I to have no personality, or rights of my own? Where is all the thrill of laboring together for the kingdom? How does my learning to bake, cook, and clean—and submit to my unfair husband—fit in with the 'glorious end-time vision of the church?'" Again, there was only a response of silence from my God to my frustrated questionings.

"Well, if you loved me as Christ loved the church, maybe I'd be able to submit to you better," I angrily lashed out at Charles after another one of our little disagreements. "And besides, some of your demands are ridiculous. What are you trying to do, completely change my personality? I won't have it, do you hear, I simply won't have it!"

Charles looked at me a little hurt, as well as a little impatiently. "Well, this is not getting us anywhere," he replied. "You will either submit to me as the Bible says, and we'll walk together in serving Him, or you'll have to lag behind. You will not hinder me from serving the Lord as He has called me to do!"

"Hinder you? Hinder you! Why it's you who's hindering me! My spiritual life has been reduced to zero ever since we've been married."

"Well, if you learned to have a 'meek and quiet spirit' perhaps God would hear you."

"Honestly, you're impossible! And it's not fair!" I stormed out of our bedroom and fell onto the living room couch, heaving with deep sobs. "What has gone wrong? Who is right, him or me? No, I know I'm right. I will not let him make a dishrag out of me!" I cried myself to sleep that night, choosing to lie on the small, uncomfortable couch rather than share the same bed with an unreasonable, dictatorial husband.

The sun reflecting brightly off the frozen snow outside awakened me as it radiantly shone through our living room window onto my face. Through swollen eyes I looked at the wall clock—eight-thirty. I couldn't remember how long I had cried before I fell asleep. I quietly tiptoed to the back bedroom and took a peek inside. The bed was made, and the back door was unlocked. Charles had obviously already left—without a word. A wave of weariness and despair swept over me. I walked back into the kitchen and put on the flame under the tea kettle. Dejectedly stirring a spoon in my coffee cup, I put my head on the table and cried once again. "O Lord, help me. Forgive me where I've been wrong. You have always been my Helper and my Friend. Please speak to me. Lord, I'm desperate. Honestly, Lord, I love You, I love my husband, I love Your church. Please help me. How did things get so mixed up?"

For the first time in a long while I felt the presence of the Lord with me. And as usual, I knew light would come to me from His Word. I decided to read again the passages relevant to marriage. After reading Ephesians 5, I turned to 1 Peter 3. As I started reading the third chapter, it appeared from the wording in verse 1—"In like manner . . . "—that it was very important to read chapter two also. When I came to verse 23 of that chapter it was as if I had never seen those words before: "Who, when he was reviled, reviled not again; when He suffered, he threatened not; but *committed himself to him that judgeth righteously*" (1 Pet. 2:23). Another meaning for the word righteously is fairly. Yes, that was an important point. "Lord," I sighed, "this is all too lopsided. Charles has to change too. You know that some of his demands are not fair. When is *he* going to change?" After a while I just sat quietly rereading 1 Peter, chapters two and three.

"My daughter, your actions have shown just how insecure you are in My love, and in My ability to see to it that you are treated fairly. You have been defending yourself, and maintaining your rights so loudly that I can't get a word in edgewise."

"O Lord, You're so right! I've been so afraid that I'd lose my identity. I felt so sorry for myself because Charles was being so unfair in his demands. Lord, I really have been afraid that if *I* didn't maintain my legitimate rights, no one else would. Forgive me, Lord, for not trusting You. Thank You that You alone judge all situations fairly. O Father, thank You that Charles is Your son. I am sorry I have hindered Your work in both our lives through my stubbornness. Deliver me from the fear that if I didn't show him where he was wrong, no one else would. O thank You, my dear Father, that You are his Father as well as mine. Thank You that You are able to speak to both of us. And if You want to change me first, I yield to Your justice and fairness."

Something broke inside of me that morning. As God continued to speak to me from His Word, it was like being washed afresh on the inside. He had revealed the stubbornness of my heart; and as I repented before Him, the warmth of His love began to melt the coldness of my heart.

Before I realized it, it was almost noon. "Oh dear Lord, keep Charles away just a little longer so I can get both myself and our little home back in order. Lord, You show me what will please him. Make me sensitive to dust those places up high that he'll see the first, and please help me to cream the peas tonight like his mom does. And what should I wear? O Lord, You lead me!" How good it was to feel once more the presence of the Lord! Around three-thirty, I heard the little brown VW pull up in front of the mobile home. Somewhat nervously I sprayed on some perfume, and put the final touches to my hair. With a slight hesitation Charles walked through the living room door, clutching a small red rose in his hand.

"I do love you, Dotty."

"Oh, Charles, I am sorry. I do love you, and thank God for you." I sobbed again in his arms, but this time from happiness and not frustration.

The adjustments to one another would be many through the years. But I had learned a life-changing principle. Regardless who is right or who is wrong, the principles of His kingdom stand eternal. "He giveth more grace. Wherefore he saith, God resisteth the proud, but giveth grace unto the humble. Submit yourselves therefore to God. Resist the devil, and he will flee from you" (James 4:6-7).

Interestingly, through the years, as we both became more secure in our Father's love and in our love for one another, we experienced increasingly the freedom of Paul's statement: "Submitting yourselves *one to another* in the fear of God" (Eph. 5:21). And yes, Charles would change too. Little did I then know some of the traumatic experiences which lay before us which would help bring about these changes. But during the next years I would observe Charles becoming more and more molded into the likeness of Him who is meek and lowly of heart.

Thank You, Father, that Your ways and Your laws are given not to bind, inhibit or destroy us, but to free us to love and to enjoy You and all that You have given us.

16

The Death of a Vision

Hear my cry, O God; attend unto my prayer.
From the end of the earth will I cry unto thee,
when my heart is overwhelmed: lead me to the
rock that is higher than I.

(Ps. 61:1-2)

"Charles, it sure seems that this is an answer to prayer. I am almost overwhelmed! Whoever thought we would find ourselves in the restaurant business?"

"Well, Dotty, the Lord knows our need for an independent economic base. Just think how we can help support some of the emerging brethren!" Charles enthusiastically replied. "These little groups are so young and so fragile at this time that the Lord must supply something to allow us to travel anywhere without, at this time, having to look to the little groups for financial assistance."

I could hardly believe what all was happening!

"How many restaurants did you say you have now opened?" my dad asked in amazement.

"Papa, it's the seventh one. Come up for the summer, and bake for us."

"Dotty, you know I'll be there. I really enjoy working in the baking department." (Dad had been trained in Europe as a professional baker and cake decorator.) "But, I don't know, don't you people think you're going a little

81

too fast? How can you open seven restaurants in such a few years with hardly any money to work with?"

"Well, Papa, there *are* a few problems, but it'll all work out. This new restaurant will help stabilize the others a little more," I naively responded to my father's conservative and cautious observations.

"Lord, I'm beginning to wonder about all this. It's challenging to be involved in the business world, but I feel like I'm in a spiritual vacuum. You seem so far away at times. We still talk about the restoration of Your church, but we now have so little time to really give ourselves to Your work." A strange foreboding fear came over me as the next thoughts ran confusedly through my mind. "And Charles—O Lord, he appears to be so different lately. He's becoming almost a stranger to me. He's more quiet than usual, and also more irritable. And how angry he is with me for having gained those thirty pounds over the past few years! You know I gained almost all of it the first year we were in the restaurant business, and Lord, nothing I do works in keeping it off. O Lord, I'm afraid, but I don't really know about what." And so once again I sensed I was in a spiritual desert. Somehow, I also came to know instinctively that what was happening in our lives was not good at all. Charles and I were losing touch with each other. He was gone so much in setting up the restaurants. And when he *was* home he was so very greatly engrossed in trying to get the general business office to run more smoothly.

"Dotty, I'm really concerned for Charles," one of our local brothers hesitantly blurted out as he stood in our kitchen. My heart must have stood still for a moment. Why would such dread sweep over me at times? I put the iron down, realizing that I had almost burned my blouse. Any day now we would be expecting our second child. Laura—who had been born three years before—was an absolute delight to us, and even in the midst of this present turmoil of business and personal pressure, we were still very much looking forward to the birth of our second child.

"Yes, I'm sensing something is wrong, but let's just pray for him." I desperately wanted to change the subject.

The brother stood and looked intently at me for a few seconds. "I guess all we *can* do right now *is* pray," he replied.

When I attempted to discuss with Charles my afternoon conversation with the local brother, he responded sharply and defensively. I said no more. That night I buried my head in the pillow and very silently wept. "O God, help us, help us. What is wrong, Lord? Why do I feel so afraid?"

"Dotty, the Lord awakened me in the middle of the night with such a burden for Charles that all I could do was cry out to the Lord in strong intercessions. In addition, the Lord showed me that He was going to deliver Charles completely from something which has plagued him periodically over the years." A ray of hope seemed to sweep over me as Wes spoke. Little did I realize, though, the anguish which lay before us in the tremendous personal struggle Charles would soon undergo. Everything was at stake: our marriage, our economics, and especially our whole walk before the Lord.

Some ten years after this period of spiritual and moral defeat, Charles was to write a little testimony touching on what had happened. I will let him describe in his own words something of the situation:

Nearly ten years ago now I passed through an experience in which I learned for myself the reality of the precious Fatherhood of my God. I had walked through a dark valley of sin and despair and disillusionment and defeat. I had fallen flat on my face and virtually saw no hope for myself. I closed my Bible and could not pray. I saw the purposes of God ended in my life. As the days wore on, my dear wife became greatly alarmed for me; and one day I found the following note lying on my closed Bible (which note I still keep as a sacred remembrance): "Dear Son, please talk with Me! Sincerely, your heavenly Father, known to most as 'God'! P.S. You could at least listen while I talk."

As I today read over Dotty's note, I still recall how oddly I was struck by the wording of it. I had never before really thought of God in that light. To me He was a stern, exacting judge. He was hardly my Father and surely not my "Dad." I guess I knew, theoretically, that "Dad" was the meaning of the Aramaic word *abba*. I guess I knew vaguely that the stern Pharisees, though they used this word in their homes with their children and their fathers, would never use *abba* in their synagogues for their God, since He could never be that to them. I guess I knew too, that Jesus, in His care-free, loving relationship with His Father, was the first one to coin the name "Dad" for Him (Mark 14:36). I guess I knew as well that this is the first word breathed into the spirit of every fresh, untainted, newborn child of God (Gal. 4:6; Rom. 8:15). But to me God had been at the most my judge—just waiting for me to sin and to fail, that He might destroy me forever in His holy judgment. And, not surprisingly, just as I had visualized Him to be toward me, so I had all too often been toward others who had failed of the grace of God. Stern views of God produce stern Pharisees, I have learned. Evangelical Pharisees. Pentecostal Pharisees. Charismatic Pharisees. End-time Pharisees. But Pharisees, nonetheless.

In the very midst of my anguish nearly ten years ago, a rather strange thing happened. My little daughter, Laura Lea, then about three, began writing on the wall with her crayons! (Now when I was single, that was one thing I had vowed would never happen with any of my children. They would never write on the walls with crayons!) And so I severely warned Laura of the consequence of her actions, only to find that the next time she did it, she wrote on the bedspread with her crayons! And I was furious. I thrashed her; I broke all the crayons in half and slammed the door behind me. She soon followed me into the living room where I lay stretched out on the carpet brooding. Failing to get my attention by her whimpering, she then came quietly over to where I lay and put her head close by my heart and just sobbed quietly. In that instant a flood of compassion filled my heart for this, my erring child. And in that instant my God spoke to me, in almost audible tones: "Even so do I love you!" At first I could not believe it! Could it ever be that God felt such compassion, such pity, such tenderness for *me*, His erring child? I stood up and walked through the house with tears streaming down my face—God was my Dad! God was my Dad! God was my Dad! I had discovered my Father!

And so, gentlest Father, we bow in worship before You. Thank You for taking the fragmented pieces of our life, and with great tenderness reassembling them. We love You, our Father, and delight to be Yours.

17

Beauty for Ashes

The Spirit of the Lord God is upon me; because the Lord hath anointed me to preach good tidings unto the meek; he hath sent me to bind up the brokenhearted, to proclaim liberty to the captives, and the opening of the prison to them that are bound; to proclaim the acceptable year of the Lord, and the day of vengeance of our God; to comfort all that mourn; to appoint unto them that mourn in Zion, to give unto them beauty for ashes, the oil of joy for mourning, the garment of praise for the spirit of heaviness; that they might be called trees of righteousness, the planting of the Lord, that he might be glorified. And they shall build the old wastes, they shall raise up the former desolations, and they shall repair the waste cities, the desolations of many generations.

(Isa. 61:1-4)

I glanced at the little wall clock in the basement of the old, wooden-framed church building—4:30 A.M.! Could it be possible that we had already been here most of the night? Never in my life had I known such confusion. Every time I now thought of the past couple of months, I just shuddered. It was as though we were in the midst of a great spiritual battle, and quite truthfully I felt we were being wiped out in the process.

I knew that these brothers with whom we were gathered in the basement loved us, but I could not understand their dealings in our lives. By 4:30 A.M. we had spent most of the night on our knees before the Lord. And often during that time I had looked at Morrie and Gisela, at Charles and the other brothers—and everyone seemed like strangers to me. My mind wandered back to recent events.

"Dotty, I am so sorry. I love you, but am not worthy of your love. In fact, I doubt whether God will ever again want to use me. I've ruined everything."

"Oh Charles, no, no! God is a redemptive God! Please, please don't give up," I cried, as I clung to Charles during those early weeks of January.

My own heart was still a turbulence of emotion. For during these months I went from feelings of deep disillusionment with my husband to some of the deepest emotions of love and compassion I had ever known. At times I wanted him to suffer because of all the hurt and pain he had brought upon us, and at other times I wanted to just hold him and cry aloud that everything would be all right. Now as the weeks passed by, we began to gain some sense of bearing in the whole situation. At the same time a few of the folks in our fellowship felt it would be good for Morrie and Gisela and Charles and I to get away for about seven days. It was mid-February, therefore, that we made plans to leave for Florida. We had also decided that on the way to the airport we would visit with some of our friends in the twin cities. They had only recently been apprised of our situation, and because they loved us and had put so much confidence in us, they were both very disappointed in us and very concerned for us.

And so in the church building basement we met with them for discussion, prayer, and weeping during nearly a full twenty-four-hour period before our departure for Florida.

Repentance was the key issue this night with our brothers. Yet I never knew there could be such confusion on this matter of repentance! It seemed to me so much easier to explain repentance and forgiveness to a complete sinner than to a believer who had sinned. "O God, what is the answer?"

It was now almost 5:00 A.M. I slowly got up from my knees and began walking upstairs. The church nursery door was open. I closed the door behind me and fell in a heap onto the floor. "O Lord, never have I felt so much alone. Everything and everyone appears so very strange to me. Even You are as a stranger to me. I am so terribly confused. God, I cry to You. I don't even know how to pray anymore, or even what I should ask of You." I stopped weeping and just sat there in absolute silence.

After a few minutes it was almost as though I were hearing an audible voice: "Open your mouth, My daughter, and I will give you the words to speak." In desperation I obediently opened my mouth, and from deep within came words which were previously unknown to me. For the next hour I spoke in many different tongues I had never previously learned. Even though I had been filled with the Spirit at age fifteen, and had often experienced His anointing to prophesy according to 1 Corinthians 12 through 14, I had, until this moment, never spoken in tongues. That night I understood firsthand Paul's statement, "I thank my God, I speak with tongues more than ye all" (1 Cor. 14:18). I was absolutely amazed at the peace and assurance which began filling my heart. As I continued to allow His Spirit to pray through me in this way, a hope began filling my heart for the first time in weeks: Jesus Christ is alive! He would see us through!

The redemptive solution to sin and failure in God's people is never easy. The breaking of God's laws—whether done by unbelievers or believers—always brings hard consequences. And so for us these months were extremely difficult ones, in the midst of which I was also to miscarry what would have been our third child—a boy.

God was doing a depth of cleansing within us which had never before been done. And this continued even upon our return from Florida.

"Dotty, do you ever think you might be acting a little self-righteous?" Morrie asked.

"Self-righteous? No, I don't. I just don't think this whole thing is fair," I defensively responded.

"What you are saying is that you didn't deserve these problems?"

"Well, yes, I suppose you could say that. Yes, you're right, I *don't* deserve all this. I got married because God led me to. I married someone I loved with all my heart, and together we were going to build His church. But because of all this mess, I doubt whether God will ever use us again." Now I began to really cry, and soon Gisela was crying with me.

"Dotty, in all you are saying you still seem to lack a comprehension of the grace of God to redeem," Morrie gently and yet firmly responded.

Well, even if he were right, I was nonetheless hurting! How I longed for an objective word of comfort from someone who was more removed from the whole situation. Somehow down deep, I guess I felt I deserved some words of comfort.

"Dotty, the Lord has given me a word for you," Wes's

voice enthusiastically sounded through the phone. My heart leaped. Wes was one of our local elders. He had been a rock of strength to us during the past months.

"If thou draw out thy soul to the hungry, and satisfy the afflicted soul; then shall thy light rise in obscurity, and thy darkness be as the noonday," Wes confidently and slowly read from Isa. 58:10.

My heart sank in disappointment as I hung up the phone. I neither understood nor wanted a word like that! "Lord, I'm in no shape to pour out to others. I'm hurting; You need to pour out to me first," I weepingly pled before Him.

During the next few days I sought the Lord even more fervently. "Lord, please meet the need of my heart. Lord, please speak to me."

After about the third day, the Lord spoke in the depths of my spirit: "My daughter, I gave you My answer three days ago. You have more truth about My Word and My ways than a great many other people. Stop feeling sorry for yourself and begin moving in the truth of My Word regardless of your feelings; and 'then shall *thy* light rise in obscurity, and *thy* darkness be as the noonday.' "

Yes, the Lord knew I was sitting in darkness, and He also knew that the last thing I needed was pity. I needed to forget about myself and begin to concentrate on Him who is the same yesterday, today, and forever. I needed to declare His faithfulness to others regardless of how I felt. And so I began to reach out hesitantly to others again. As I commenced to speak the truth of God's Word, my own life began to experience the comforting rays of God's love, warmth, and healing!

It was early April. And although it was still cold outside, there were some early signs of spring in the air.

The doorbell rang. As I opened the door I was greeted not only by the refreshing fragrance of an early spring rain but also by the strong fragrance of Jesus' life as it was flowing through a man of God. There before me stood Bob Sadler, a beloved black brother from Ohio, whom we had known for years. (Bob was called home to glory in the summer of 1976. His dynamic life story has been told in a biography of him by Marie Chapian.*)

"Sister Dorothy, the Lord spoke to me in Ohio a while back and said that brother Charles and sister Dorothy needed me, and here I am." My heart rejoiced in anticipation as I invited this man of God into our home to spend a few days with us, for he would often break forth into praises to the Lord at the slightest nudgings. His endless stories of how the Lord would lead him to the poor, needy, and destitute of our society deeply stirred our hearts. The compassion and joy of our Lord tumbled out of his life, and blessed everyone around him. Our little, brown-eyed, three-year-old, Laura loved to sit on his lap and discuss with him why Jesus had made the inside of his hands white and the outside of his hands black.

"Brother Sadler, breakfast is almost ready," I called downstairs to where he was staying. (Charles and I by this time were living in a large house in Grand Rapids, Minnesota, having moved here in 1966 from our mobile home in Cohasset five miles away.)

"Not this morning, sister Dorothy; the Lord and I are having such a good time, I do believe I'll tarry a little longer before Him."

I was standing by our sink just finishing the morning

The Emancipation of Robert Sadler (Minneapolis: Bethany Press, 1975) dishes when brother Sadler came upstairs. He sat down on our green provincial sofa located in front of our large living-room picture window. "Sister Dorothy, when you are finished, come in and sit by me for a while." I sat down on the couch, and before he even spoke, the tears silently fell down my face.

"Yes, yes, sister Dorothy, let them come. For the Lord shall indeed restore to you 'beauty for ashes.' He has not forgotten you. For surely you shall find that that which the enemy meant for evil to you, God shall turn around and use for your good. Only trust Him, child; He is far from finished in your lives. The joy of His salvation shall be abundantly restored to your household, and you shall again labor in the vineyard of your God."

I received these comforting words into my spirit just as a dry sponge hungrily absorbs the water around it. "Oh, thank You, Jesus, for Your marvelous grace and mercy!" I cried aloud from joy.

Yes, the Lord knew we had miserably failed Him. He also knew more accurately than anyone else that apart from His triumphant grace operative in our lives, we would have been destroyed as a couple and as fruitful servants in His kingdom. In His faithfulness He knew when to be firm, and when to give not pity—which could further destroy us—but true comfort.

We emerged out of the despair and despondency of those months much humbled, much pruned, and much transformed. As husband and wife we came into an honesty and transparency between us which drew us even closer. As servants of the Lord we saw in Him anew the truth of the statement: "Mercy rejoiceth against judgment" (James 2:13).

Thank You, Father, that Your judgments are always redemptive. Thank You that Your mercy doesn't overlook sin, but that it causes You to deal with it in order to transform us into the beautiful likeness of Your Son. What a relief to know we can depend on You when everything else seems to be crumbling. And thank You, Lord, that from the ashes around us You are able to bring forth the beauty of Your holiness.

18

The Opening of a New Door

*It is of the Lord's mercies that we are not
consumed, because his compassions fail not.
They are new every morning: great is thy
faithfulness.*

(Lam. 3:22-23)

It was a typically crisp, cold northern Minnesota
evening! A little more than a year had passed since we
experienced that crisis in our lives which had almost
destroyed us. We had done virtually nothing in terms of
public ministry during this time. Actually we were still a
little uncertain as to whether or not God even wanted to
use us again in that capacity. The vision for the restoration
of His church yet burned within our hearts, but what
our part was in that restoration was presently quite dim
to us.

The phone rang! I could tell from the way Charles was
speaking that it was a long distance call. After a few
minutes he cupped the receiver, saying, "We're being
invited to speak at a meeting in Lincoln. What do you
think?" I shrugged my shoulders. All desire to travel,
speak, or to do any public ministry at all had left us both.
Besides, the restaurants were demanding almost full
attention at this time. I picked up the extension phone.

"Look, you know I know everything that has happened
in your lives during this past couple of years. But as some

94

of us have been praying down here, we just feel that the Lord is saying you are now to begin sharing again the word He has placed on your hearts. You have gone through the fire so that you might be purified, not that you might be destroyed from His purposes in this hour." The voice of our longtime friend, Kencil, came over the phone with firm and zealous conviction. And so the arrangements were made for us to go the next month to Lincoln, Nebraska.

The snow was sparkling and crunchy under our feet. Charles gently carried our sleepy, lovely four-and-a-half-year-old daughter into the car. Laura was to travel with us, while our precious Dianna—who was now one-and-a-half-years old—would stay with our dependable and faithful Grandma Frieda.

"Now just you don't worry. You know I love these girls as if they were my own. Dianna will be just fine. The Lord give you a real good blessing while you're gone." Frieda hugged me as I a little hesitantly closed the door behind me.

We began driving silently across the beautiful snow-laden back roads toward the main road. Just before us on the horizon were the first early signs of a new day beginning to dawn. The silence both without and within the car seemed to be pregnant with the presence of the Lord. Quietly Charles and I began to sing an old familiar hymn:

> When morning gilds the sky,
> My heart awaking cries,
> May Jesus Christ be praised.

It was almost as if I could reach out and touch Him, so strong was His presence with us that crisp, early winter morning. Deep within me stirred part of a verse from Rev. 3:8: "Behold, I have set before thee an open door, and no man can shut it."

I quietly wept as I sat listening to Charles give his testimony of the Lord's dealings and leadings in his life. It was such a long time since I had last heard him publicly share from the Scriptures. That same anointing which had first drawn me to him as a twelve-year-old was still upon him, but with a far greater authority. Charles wove into his testimony the account in Joshua 7 of Achan's sin of attempting to hide an "accursed thing" from the Lord and His people, and the terrible consequences of such hiding. As Charles began declaring the mercy, forgiveness, and Lordship of Jesus in our lives, it felt as though the presence of the Holy Spirit was hovering just above us—like heavy rain clouds on a summer day. Before he was even able to complete his message, an older brother jumped to his feet and gave a dynamic message in tongues. As the interpretation came for all to heed the words which were being spoken and to yield totally to the Lord's dealing in our lives, the rain from heaven began to fall. I could not remember when I had witnessed such repentance and confession. People began flocking up front, falling to their knees, weeping and seeking the face of the Lord. As I joined Charles to pray for some of these people, a compassion began filling my heart—for these, God's people, whom I had never before known. I could almost see the Great Shepherd himself walking in the midst of His sheep. Deep within me I could hear Him say: "If you love Me, you will feed My sheep."

As I knelt down to pray with the different ones who were seeking the Lord, my heart was especially drawn to one young woman. She knelt with her head almost in her lap, sobbing in repentance before the Lord. As I gently placed my hand upon her head, there stirred within me such a strong desire for the Lord to comfort her that I also began to weep. Again, the voice of the Lord spoke: "Open your mouth, My daughter, and I will speak to this My child." I began speaking to the young woman. Never before had I known such a prophetic flow. The Bible teaches that the gift of prophecy is given to the church to bring edification, exhortation, and comfort to the people of God. It was a gift I desired from the Lord, and it appeared to flow, but not until this night had I ever known such an anointing to prophesy.

After the gathering that night, this young woman sought me out to thank me. I gave her a big hug, and said, "Thank *you!*" With a kind of puzzlement in her eyes she searched my face for some reason as to why *she* should be thanked. "Your intense longing for the Lord provoked such compassion and faith in my own heart that the prophetic word simply exploded within me. Thank *you* for allowing me to seek the Lord with you."

A new hour, a new day, and a new door had indeed been opened for us that memorable winter weekend. We returned to Grand Rapids from the experience as changed people. It was hard to understand the many reports which came back to us about lives that had been transformed as a result of our having been there, because *we* were the ones who seemed to have been the most blessed and the most transformed. The vision of His church and her triumph in these days burned even more intensely within our souls. And once more we knew we had been born to love and serve the Lord!

We returned to our own small fellowship of believers with a new hope, a renewed expectation, and an overwhelming sense of gratitude for the infinite mercy and unfailing faithfulness of our Great and Faithful High Priest, the Lord Jesus.

Father, it is an absolute delight to know You. Your ways are beyond our natural comprehension. Thank You for Your faithful dealings in our lives, and thank You that when You open a door, no man can shut it, and when You close a door, no man can open it.

19

An Eternal Lesson

*For our light affliction, which is but for a
moment, worketh for us a far more exceeding
and eternal weight of glory; while we look not
at the things which are seen, but at the things
which are not seen: for the things which are
seen are temporal; but the things which are not
seen are eternal.* (2 Cor. 4:17-18)

"God can do anything but fail!" Morrie and Gisela,
Charles and I were walking through the debris of a
southern Minnesota restaurant which had only recently
closed down, singing the refrain of this chorus. We were
desperately seeking a way to stabilize the other restaurants we had opened. Four had done very well until we
overprojected in the fifth. There was no question that
we had to divide some of the equipment from the fifth
restaurant and put it into this new one which we had just
acquired.

"O God, there is so much at stake. You know we want
to walk in integrity in the finances. Surely You'll honor
us in this venture" was our constant cry before the Lord.
As we walked through this old restaurant, we knew we
could make it work. God would help us!

We were busier than ever. The door to public ministry
had definintely reopened, the local fellowship was growing in every way, and now only the restaurants were in
need of a touch from the Lord.

"Charles, it's 2:00 A.M. Don't you think we ought to

99

quit? Morrie, you've been at it since 7:00 A.M.! How can you even see to hook up any more equipment?"

"Dotty, we need to get this place opened. So if we must work around the clock, we will have to do so." Even Gisela was on the kitchen floor, helping Morrie hook up the pipes.

Finally opening day came. We were physically exhausted, but very hopeful. This was truly an answer to our prayer. We had taken virtually no finances ourselves for months, and we just knew God would honor us. After all, His glory was at stake in this whole venture.

"Charles, what do you mean it's too late? God led us!"

"Dotty, we overexpanded too quickly; some of our business principles were totally impractical. I don't believe God overlooks unsound business principles merely because we feel we have a promise from the Bible."

"But Charles, how can this be? We worked so hard! Will we have to close all of them? Oh God, what a mess!"

"No, some of them we'll sell, and some will be closed. Then we'll have to pick up the pieces of this venture," Charles decisively responded to my more emotional outbursts.

In the midst of all this, Charles and I were scheduled for a weekend conference in Lincoln. I was to take the bus from Grand Rapids to Lincoln. It had been about three months since the Mankato restaurant—our last hope to salvage the business—had been closed. The bus I was in took the Mankato route and passed directly in front of "our" restaurant. That place represented hours upon hours of our most diligent labor and efforts, and there before me it was now being completely dismantled. It had looked so elegant, and was full of so much promise. A deep pain shot through my insides as I peered through the bus window and watched what was happening to all the desperate labor of our hands!

"O God, how could this have happened?" I cried before the Lord as the tears flowed profusely down my cheeks.

The presence of the Lord engulfed me at that moment, and it was as if I were totally alone in that bus. "My child, weep not for what you have produced in the natural. Instead, make sure that in the day in which you stand in My presence, your spiritual labors will not in like manner be so easily dismantled." A passage of Scripture began to fill my mind from 1 Cor. 3:10-15. I read and reread the following verses:

> According to the grace of God which is given unto me, as a wise masterbuilder, I have laid the foundation, and another buildeth thereon. But let every man take heed how he buildeth thereupon. For other foundation can no man lay than that is laid, which is Jesus Christ. Now if any man build upon this foundation gold, silver, precious stones, wood, hay, stubble; every man's work shall be made manifest: for the day shall declare it, because it shall be revealed by fire; and the fire shall try every man's work of what sort it is. If any man's work abide which he hath built thereupon, he shall receive a reward. If any man's work shall be burned, he shall suffer loss: but he himself shall be saved; yet so as by fire.

"Will what you're building in My kingdom stand the test of My fire, My daughter?"

"O Lord, I don't know. O Lord, how terrible I feel watching my earthly labors crumble, but how would I feel watching my spiritual labors burned to ashes? Lord, teach me to build not with hay, wood, and stubble, but with gold, silver, and precious stones."

"Precious stones are found in the hard places, often in the dark places, My child. Hay and wood are easily found; there's comparatively little effort involved in finding these materials. But there is a cost involved in building My house. You must deny yourself. You must esteem others higher than yourself. You must be willing to step aside so another can be recognized and appreciated. You must be glad for others to receive the credit for something your prayers actually brought into existence. You must be a servant to My people, and be willing to do the most menial task in order to see them enhanced. Remember that you live to see the gold of My nature and character formed in others, and that I am meek and lowly of heart. My church shall come forth with great signs and wonders in the days to come, but remember that My purpose is to have a Bride without spot and wrinkle. I *will* have a holy people. So expect My fire to touch not only your actions but also your motives, since only the pure in heart shall see God. For I desire that you would see Me, for as you behold Me in My glory, you shall be changed into My image and likeness."

I sat in the bus, quietly weeping for joy. The hours of travel were only like minutes as wave upon wave of His illumination and presence swept over me. The Scriptures were incredibly alive as He quickened passage upon passage to me concerning building in His kingdom with precious stones.

Even though Charles had only been gone for a few days, I longed to be with him again. I was picked up at the Lincoln bus depot and taken directly to the meeting where Charles was already speaking. How precious these people had become to us during these months. In fact, we became so engrossed in the lives of some of the believers there that Charles and I smiled at one another as we exhaustedly collapsed in bed, realizing we had not even had a moment alone to share together. But there was always tomorrow!

We were both scheduled to share at a breakfast for leaders and their wives in the morning. "This week the Lord has been speaking to me from the passage in 1 Cor. 3:10-15, on the necessity of building not with hay, wood, or stubble, but building with gold, silver, and precious stones. Leaders in the House of God, He is more interested in what we *are* than in what we *do!*" I could hardly believe what I was hearing. My heart beat with such joy and wonder as I heard my husband share almost the identical word the Lord had spoken to me in the bus the day before.

It would take us years to work through the consequences of our zealous but unwise business venture. We gradually realized that what had begun as an enterprise to enhance the kingdom became a snare of worldly entanglement to us. And the Father, in His wisdom, allowed the earthly kingdom to collapse so that we might undistractedly attend to the affairs of His spiritual kingdom.

Thank You, Father, for so faithfully dealing in our lives. Thank You for pruning us from those temporal involvements which dull us to the eternal realities of Your kingdom.

20

Watch Out, Here Come the Jesus People!

Remember ye not the former things, neither consider the things of old. Behold, I will do a new thing; now it shall spring forth; shall ye not know it? I will even make a way in the wilderness, and rivers in the desert.

(Isa. 43:18-19)

Peanut butter all over the cupboard and counters again! Some more dirty dishes in the sink! Boy, it sure seemed easier to feel spiritual while at a meeting with other believers than it was here in my own kitchen. What's all that racket downstairs? Oh, no, not the drums and bass guitars again! Don't they ever get tired of playing some of that music? How are my girls going to get to sleep with all that noise going on? Lord, how did we end up with all these guys living with us?

My mind went over the events of the past few months. Since that memorable weekend in Lincoln, the blessings of the Lord had been released in abundance upon us as a fellowship. When we moved from our small mobile home to our house in Grand Rapids, the small fellowship began meeting in our larger living room. As we grew in number, we knocked out all the walls in our walk-in basement. We could now comfortably seat about seventy-five persons.

I woke up one Sunday morning during these months experiencing a very strong urge to pray. This desire to pray became all the more intense during the morning gathering. After the gathering, I knew I needed to spend more time in prayer.

"Gisela, drop what you're doing. I know Frieda, Pearl, and Selma are praying at Emma's house this afternoon, so please come with me."

"Dotty, I'm feeling the same desire to pray. Yes, come for me as soon as you can," Gisela responded to my phone conversation.

As we walked into Emma's bright cheery home, the four women were already praying. Gisela and I simply fell to our knees and joined in with them.

"Lord Jesus, move upon the young people in this town."

"Lord, pour out Your Spirit upon them. Help them to see the dead-end street which sin leads to."

"Jesus, draw by Your Spirit these young ones to Yourself. Redeem them and cause them to live fruitful lives."

Never before had I experienced such intensity of intercession. We hadn't known what we were going to pray for that afternoon at Emma's house until we actually began to pray. Then all we could ask Him for was to touch the lives of the young people. During the next few months many of us gathered spontaneously together simply to pray.

"Oh, great! Will Tim and Dave be home from the university? Good, then you'll all be up for the Easter convocation in our home!" I excitedly overheard Charles talking to Freeman and Buzz from Ashland, Nebraska. The Easter conference was only a week away. Already we had a real sense of expectancy. God had something special in mind.

During the middle of the service on Good Friday evening, Tim and Dave expressed a very strong urge to minister to the young people on the streets. "We're going to go to some of the pizza parlors and just tell the kids that Jesus Christ is alive. Maybe some of you could pray for us as we go," Tim suggested, as he and Dave left for downtown Grand Rapids. Later that evening they returned from town with a small group of young people.

And that was the beginning! The conference officially closed with lunch on Sunday afternoon. For the remainder of the afternoon, a few of us worked together getting our house back in order. We were just getting ready to sit down and enjoy a quiet evening at home when at about eight-fifteen, young people began streaming into the house through almost every door.

"Say, we hear something unusual is going on here."

"What's all this stuff about Jesus?"

"Can we come in and rap a while?"

"Dotty, call Morrie and Jim, and whoever else is home, and ask them to come and help us. And tell them to hurry, there must be more than fifty kids here already," Charles called to me as he began assembling everyone in our walk-in basement. When I finally got back downstairs the air was already blue with smoke. Near the bottom of the stairs sat a rather slight but cute young girl with large, expressive brown eyes. We began talking together.

"You know this is Easter Sunday?"

"So?"

"Well, that means we're celebrating the fact that Jesus Christ is alive."

"How do you know He is?"

"Because I gave Him my life many years ago, and He and I have spent much time together ever since."

"You're crazy! You mean you really believe that?"

This lovely young gal was now both trembling and weeping.

"Yes, I really believe in Him! Would you like to also?"

With an intensity I hadn't anticipated, she cried, "Yes, yes, I would!" Before the night was over, Cathy experienced for herself the reality of the One who boldly declared, "Fear not; I am the first and the last: I am he that liveth, and was dead; and, behold, I am alive for evermore, Amen; and have the keys of hell and of death" (Rev. 1:17-18).

For the next two weeks our house was open day and night to these young people. Parents, teachers, and other pastors called to ask what was happening. We called upon a number of other local people to come and help us—this was a little too big for us to handle alone. We had nightly sessions with kids who wanted to "rap" about Jesus.

One evening as I sat on the staircase listening to the different conversations, a passage from the Gospels came to me very strongly: "Whosoever doth not bear his cross, and come after me, cannot be my disciple. For which of you, intending to build a tower, sitteth not down first, and counteth the cost, whether he have sufficient to finish it?" (Luke 14:27-28).

"Say, kids, you know the Lord doesn't only want to zap you with a good feeling. He wants your life. He is your Savior and *Lord*. When you come to Him, He's going to take the reins of your life."

I quickly realized that a sensitive area had been touched. A weeding out began taking place as the Lordship of Jesus was presented. Over the next few months we would clearly see demonstrated before us the truth of the parable of the sower and the seed. For the seed of the gospel was to fall on the soil of all types of human hearts. It was also to meet with all the varying responses found in Mark 4:1-20.

Our lives were quite different as a result of those days. Soon young people from many different places heard about our fellowship, and came to spend a season with us. Many of them came from the hippie background. Here they were, "street people" come to live with us "straight people," and, in many ways quite "square people" at that.

At one point we had up to nine young men living with us. And me? Well, at first, it was very exhilarating. But then the realities of constant cooking, cleaning, and washing began to catch up with me. Perhaps more than anything, I suffered from the lack of privacy for myself and my family.

One morning I started to get up out of bed, but simply couldn't. Physically, emotionally, and spiritually, I was too exhausted. I sank back into the soft pillow, and just wept. Charles took but one look at me. "You will stay in bed today, the whole day."

"But the children, the cooking, the . . ."

I had not even finished the sentence when I heard the familiar voice of one of the young gals in our fellowship. I called to her, and when she came into the bedroom she gave me a hug and said, "Somehow, I knew you needed me today. Stay in bed, I'll take care of everything." And if anyone could take care of things I knew Ann could.

It ended up that not only did I spend one day in bed but the next *three* days as well. During those days the Father dealt deeply in my life. I had been so busy trying to be spiritual that I had spent very little time listening to Him.

"Who are you trying to impress, My daughter?"

"Why, Lord, I'm doing all this for You."

"Oh?"

"Well, Lord, maybe not all!"

"Oh?"

"OK, Lord, I guess what I'm really trying to do is to impress people with how spiritual I am. After all, as Charles' wife, I'm expected to be nice and spiritual."

"How have you fared?"

"Oh, just terrible, Lord; it's so hard trying to be something I'm not." A verse from Ephesians kept coming to me: "Speaking the truth in love, [you] may grow up into him in all things, which is the head, even Christ" (Eph. 4:15).

I reflected on some of my recent experiences.

"Dotty, you don't mind if we come up and study in the living room now, do you?"

"Can we use the dining room table so that we can lay out our Bibles, notes, and commentaries?"

"Say, Dotty, do you mind doing this load of wash for me; I simply don't have time now."

"Boy, are we hungry; sorry we got home so late. Is there anything left to eat?"

And so it went. I would get everything cleaned up and look forward to some minutes of quiet, only to have everybody upstairs again, eating and fellowshiping. Obviously the "spiritual" thing to say was, "Oh, sure, just use and do whatever you desire. This is the Lord's house, you know." But meanwhile, within I would be battling attitudes of disappointment and resentment.

During those three days of blessed collapse the Lord showed me I needed to be real and honest. In many ways I was driving myself to be and do what He had never asked of me. In other ways He also made it very clear that for much of my labor I already had my reward, for I wasn't doing my "good works in secret unto the Father" (Matt. 6:6). Actually I was enjoying the praise, applause and sympathy of other people. "Oh, sister Dorothy, we simply do not know how you do all this. It's just marvelous." How subtle and deceitful the human heart is. Yet the Father is most faithful to allow all deceit and fraud of our hearts to be exposed so that we can repent and be changed!

He dealt with me so very tenderly and yet almost ruthlessly during those three days. I knew it was time to grow up in Him in a new way. I needed to know that He saw my heart and understood me at all times. Amazingly, even though He knew me so completely, He still loved and accepted me! He wanted me to be real in the midst of His people. No need for masks or pretenses of spirituality. Simply Him living His life through me.

What a relief it was to realize that my desire for some time alone with my daughters and husband was not necessarily selfish. Or that to request that the noise of the "mini-orchestra" downstairs be kept to certain times of the day would not necessarily cause them not to like me anymore. Or that placing the simple requirements upon our "expanding family"—such that, if for example, one ate the peanut butter and jelly sandwiches one also cleaned up after oneself—would not necessarily convey that I was unspiritual. What a relief to be able "to speak the *truth* in *love.*" It was then that I received a release to actually love and care for His people in a way I couldn't before when I was trying so hard to impress people with how spiritual I was. Why, I found that I was in reality enjoying these young people! As we learned to live in an atmosphere of truth, order, and openness in our home, I found that not only was I serving them but also they were imparting to me truths which were of eternal value.

Father, we love You! Thank You so much that
You are committed to making us real men and

110

women of faith, and not some plastic imitations. Thank You that You really are the Vine, and we are but the branches. We are learning, Lord, that without You we can do and be nothing. Thanks for being so patient as we're learning.

21

Who, Me, Disappointed?

For the scripture saith, Whosoever believeth on him shall not be ashamed.[1]

(Rom. 10:11)

The huge picture window in our bedroom emitted only a dull, dreary light. As I slowly opened my eyes I knew I was feeling very poorly physically. In fact, my skin hurt even if I moved but a little.

For years I had sought the Lord on the issue of physical healing for the eczema with which I still had periodic battles. I prayed, fasted, claimed, was anointed, took authority over, received prayer for, and followed whatever other counsel I was given on the subject of healing. Frequently I found myself more exhausted and weaker in faith after these experiences than I had been before. Even the testimonies of those who had been healed began to cause an inner response of resentment and bitterness. Deep within I found myself thinking, "Well, I'm sure glad He's doing something for everybody else. Am I not serving Him, and knocking myself out in His service? Why doesn't He answer *me?* . . . Lord, if You

---

[1] The Amplified Bible translates this passage: "The Scripture says, No man who believes in Him—who adheres to, relies on and trusts in Him—will [ever] be put to shame or be disappointed."

112

healed me I could serve You even better!" But it appeared He was totally unimpressed with my bargaining pleas.

During recent months my disillusionment and frustration over not being able to "appropriate what was rightfully mine as a believer" began to affect negatively my entire walk before the Lord. Sometimes I wished I had not even heard of divine healing!

As I awoke this particular morning I knew my skin was inflamed and infected worse than ever. I continued lying in bed with the tears streaming down my face. "O God, I'm so tired of trying. Where *are* You in all of this?" Then, almost as if emblazoned upon my mind, I saw the words

Blessed is he who is not offended in Me.

I never recalled having understood that phrase and wasn't sure even where it was found. My attention was arrested by the word "offended." I had read in another context that the word "offended" carried with it the connotation of "disappointment."

I took my Bible from the shelf. Finally I found the passage. It was in Luke 7:18-23. Slowly I read the verses.

And the disciples of John shewed him of all these things. And John calling unto him two of his disciples sent them to Jesus, saying, Art thou he that should come? or look we for another? . . . And in that same hour he cured many of their infirmities and plagues, and of evil spirits; and unto many that were blind he gave sight. Then Jesus answering said unto them, Go your way, and tell John what things ye have seen and heard; how that the blind see, the lame walk, the lepers are cleansed, the deaf hear, the dead are raised, to the poor the gospel is preached. And blessed is he, whosoever shall not be offended in me.

It was almost as though I could feel what John the

Baptist was feeling on that particular day of his life. He had asked his disciples to find out whether Jesus really was the Christ. What had happened to John between the day he had so boldly proclaimed Jesus' identity at His baptism to this day when he now was obviously not so certain? To put it quite simply, he now found himself in a dark, damp, dreary prison. (I began seeing how I too had become filled with doubt as I found myself in a "prison" of unforeseen circumstances with few or no answers from the Lord.)

I could almost "see" the thoughts of John at this time! Word had just come to him about Jesus' raising the dead on two different occasions, and there John was—sitting in prison! Now anybody knows it is a far simpler task to open prison doors than it is to raise the dead. Had Jesus forgotten about His beloved cousin languishing in prison?

Jesus' response to the question of John's disciples was to heal—and to make whole—many lives right before these disciples' eyes. Tell this to John, He told them, adding, "And blessed is he, whosoever shall not be offended in me."

In some ways Jesus' response was pouring salt into an open wound. Perhaps there was a great struggle within John's soul. "Lord, if You do *those* things, then why am I here in *these* circumstances? Wouldn't it honor You more for me to continue preaching the Word? Have You forgotten me in the midst of all this miraculous activity?"

I lay still for quite a while allowing this illumination from His Word to saturate my very thirsty soul. Again the Lord spoke quietly within me: "My daughter, no matter what I do or don't do, your faith is based upon My character and not upon My activity. Regardless of circumstances, I have promised to 'never leave thee, nor forsake thee' " (Heb. 13:5).

After a little time I opened my Amplified Bible and read and reread its rendering of Luke 7:23: "And blessed—happy . . . and to be envied—is he who takes no offense in Me and who is not hurt or resentful or annoyed or repelled or made to stumble, [whatever may occur]."

How absolutely relevant this Bible verse was to my present situation. Without consciously realizing it, I had become somewhat hardened and cold towards the Lord because I felt He had overlooked my need. Yes, I *had* become disappointed in God! As I grew increasingly honest before Him, I realized I subtly felt He owed it to me to heal me. I shuddered at this revelation of my heart. I now wept, not because of my physical condition but because of my spiritual condition. "Forgive me, Father, cleanse my heart, and renew the fervency of my love towards You."

It was amazing! When I took my eyes off "my healing" and placed them upon the Healer, my whole attitude and outlook changed. He was faithful regardless of appearances. His love for me never changes! As I received fresh illumination of the Lord himself, renewed faith sprang up within my heart. I heard Him speak clearly in the depths of my soul: "My daughter, as you give yourself to the healing of My Body upon this earth, I shall give Myself to the healing of *your* body. Take your eyes off yourself, and place them upon Me."

Thank You, Father, that You are sovereign in all Your dealings. Thank You that You haven't given us formulas to live by; rather, that You are our health, strength, and very life! Thank You for those experiences which shut us up to but one truth—Jesus never fails.

22

The Inspiring Audience

And these all, having obtained a good report through faith, received not the promise: God having provided some better thing for us, that they without us should not be made perfect. Wherefore seeing we also are compassed about with so great a cloud of witnesses, let us lay aside every weight, and the sin which doth so easily beset us, and let us run with patience the race that is set before us, looking unto Jesus the author and finisher of our faith.

(Heb. 11:39-12:2)

That's it. I have had it! "Lord, I have failed in this area more times than I can count now. I know harboring resentment and unforgiveness is wrong, but every time I think I have the victory something else happens; and there I am feeling and thinking the same negative thing. I'm tired of trying to overcome!"

Through tears and through deep sighs, these were my thoughts that early Saturday evening. I knew I had once again failed the Lord by indulging in resentment towards someone. For months now it was becoming clear that I was getting worse in this area: even I who had so often spoken of the need for a clean heart. Here I was struggling time and again with this bitterness and resentment. Oh (groan), sometimes it was just too hard to live this "victorious Christian life."

Rather grouchy and grumpy, I retired to my bedroom earlier than usual. It always appeared that I got more tired when I had such inner defeats. As I lay in bed half muttering to myself and half murmuring to the Lord, I could almost visualize my struggle in concrete form. I saw myself running an obstacle course. I did well until I hit a certain hurdle. Each time I hit this hurdle it would knock me down. And each time I'd get up only to have the same defeat take place again. After a while, though, I didn't even bother to get up again. On the contrary, feeling very discouraged, I began to crawl away from all the activity of running. At this juncture it became apparent that I had been running in a stadium which was filled with people. All at once the stadium became alive with people standing and others jumping to their feet and shouting: "Don't give up now, you're almost finished! The race is almost finished, just a little more and you'll win the race!"

Hebrews 11 and 12 came suddenly alive to me. For it appeared as though I could actually see in the stadium the saints who had gone before, just cheering me on.

A number of weeks before, I had read a biographical account of the life of Martin Luther's wife, Katherine. How impressed I had been with her creativity, resourcefulness, and stamina. Her ability to endure very difficult circumstances deeply inspired me. I read about her feeding numerous students and guests at her table on an almost daily basis (and without any of our modern conveniences!). How impressed I was with how often she was left to care for her children, house, and local affairs while Martin attended to some of the weightier issues of his day. Upon closing the book I was deeply grateful for Katie Luther's commitment and sacrifice in helping to restore some of what we as His church presently enjoy. She was in that great stadium of believers.

Then there was Mary, the mother of Jesus. In great detail I could still recall that one evening when we were worshiping the Lord in the basement of our home. Deep within me I could hear the Lord speaking: "I'm looking for a woman I can trust even as I was able to trust Mary." Wow, that was different! Thus far I always felt *I* had to trust *Him*, so what could He possibly mean?

I found myself wondering exactly what kind of woman the Lord would choose to bear His Son. Indeed, what *were* these people like whom God used to accomplish His purposes on earth?

I began searching the Bible in regard to Mary, and found that it revealed quite a woman. Many times her deep love for her Son sought for a way to protect Him from unpleasant situations and harsh criticisms (Mark 3:20-21, 30-35). During Jesus' years of public ministry, Mary had to learn to die daily to her own feelings and desires. She had, in fact, to learn in a practical way the reality of Jesus' teachings: "Whosoever will save his life shall lose it: and whosoever shall lose his life for my sake shall find it" (Matt. 16:25). As the resistance and opposition daily increased against her Son, there was no room for a possessive kind of love. No room for self-pity, or for resentment at His being misunderstood or rejected. Mary probably experienced these temptations with great intensity at times, but she knew her God would not tempt her above what she was able to bear. And God knew the woman whom He had chosen for this very special task of raising His Son. Mary early learned that love was no mere sentiment or vague nice feeling. Love meant involvement, sacrifice, suffering, the total giving

118

of oneself, and living in an attitude of forgiveness.

Mary's supreme test must have come as she stood at the cross watching her Son die! Perhaps here, the wisdom of God's choice is most clearly seen! There are no scenes of uncontrolled bitter hysteria. Mary was willing to look away from her own pain to the pain of Another. As she watched that for which she had lived *die*, something within her also died. Perhaps at this very moment she remembered the words of Jesus: "Verily, verily, I say unto you, Except a corn of wheat fall into the ground and die, it abideth alone: but if it die, it bringeth forth much fruit" (John 12:24). Mary's confidence was not in vain. She would soon know, with all of heaven and earth, that He who once was dead was now alive forevermore!

As I fingered through the Gospels ferreting out all I could about Mary, my eyes also discovered the following passages: "Blessed are the merciful: for they shall obtain mercy" and "Forgive us our debts, *as we* forgive our debtors" (Matt. 5:7; 6:12).

I thought of Peter, and how the Lord instructed him to forgive seventy times seven (Matt. 18:21-22). I remembered Miriam, who because of resentment towards Moses, was stricken with leprosy for seven days (Numbers 12). And I reread the description in Hebrews 11 of the believers who had lived in other periods of history.

Yes, Mary was there too in that great grandstand. Also Miriam, Sarah, Abraham, Peter, Luther, the Wesleys—the list was endless! People who throughout the ages gave all they had to see His great purposes accomplished upon the earth.

As I lay in my bed reflecting on all of this, my own problem became more and more insignificant. "O Lord, it seems far too costly to hold onto these wrong attitudes. I confess this again to You as sin, and I do repent of it. Now then, You finish the work in my heart." I fell asleep exhausted, but also quite refreshed at the realization of having such a "great cloud of witnesses" cheering me on.

Thank You, Father, for the inspiration of the lives of Your people who have gone before us. Thank You for the whole family of God in heaven and on earth. And thank You that this wider vision of your purposes helps us to deal with our day-to-day weaknesses and sins. Thank You, Lord, for cleansing us from all wrong attitudes. By Your grace, we shall love and bless even our enemies.

23

"Dominion"

For if the casting away of them [natural Israel]
be the reconciling of the world, what shall the
receiving of them be, but life from the dead?
(Rom. 11:15)

"Dotty, I simply can't get away this afternoon. Why don't you go up, meet Buck, and see if you think there is anything to these campgrounds," Charles suggested while we were eating breakfast.

It was a crisp, gorgeous autumn day! I felt exhilarated and renewed by the drive to Steamboat Lake. The leaves on the trees were already bright crimson and vivid gold. They provided an excellent background for the tall, deep-green pines which frequently lined the highway. The whole scene testified to the fact that there is beauty in change.

Buck and Gene Woodard, very dear friends of ours, had been looking for a campground to be used for youth retreats, and for the general upbuilding of God's people. Actually they were open to anything north, south, east, or west of Omaha that would be located within a five-hundred-dred-mile radius. And here we were investigating a campground in Minnesota, a mere fifty-five miles west of our home in Grand Rapids. As I pulled into the camp driveway there was a growing anticipation rising within me.

As I rounded the curve in the road and saw the outline of the lovely lake and the rugged exteriors of the brown cabins against the large white birch and green pine trees, I knew the Father had chosen this place for a very special purpose.

But the actual story of "Dominion" (that being the name we eventually assigned to the camp) began months before in Nebraska. It is in reality the story of relationships!

"Has anyone ever told you that you look and sound like Arthur Katz?"*

"Well, now that you mention it, yes, about a hundred people since I've begun ministering in the Midwest," Charles would laughingly respond to this frequent question.

"Gene, when do you think we'll get to meet my look-alike?"

"Charles, Buck and I have been trying to get you two together but you always seem to be missing one another. In God's timing I know He'll arrange a meeting," Gene responded confidently to Charles' smiling inquiry.

"Dotty, why don't we spend some time waiting on the Lord in prayer for a while this morning," Joanne suggested one day during my visit with her in her home in Omaha. The spirit of prayer was upon us, and time passed quickly as she and I prayed for many people and for many nations. As we began praying for Israel I sensed His presence upon us in an unusual way.

"Lord, thank You for pouring out Your Spirit upon people from all different groups and nations. Thank You

---

*Arthur's autobiographical story is told in *Ben Israel, an Odyssey of a Modern Jew* (Plainfield, New Jersey: Logos International, 1970).

that Your church is truly being restored in this hour. But Lord, remember, You died to bring forth a church made up of both Jew and Gentile. Lord Jesus, move powerfully in this decade to bring the Jewish people to the realization that the Messiah has indeed come. God, pour out Your Spirit upon the natural seed of David. Incorporate them into the House You are building in this hour." And so we prayed for a long period of time. In the midst of these prayers we were also asking the Lord to bless and anoint the lives of Art and Inger Katz as they shared the good news of Jesus especially to the Jewish people.

Once more, quietly from within came His voice to my spirit: "The lives of your family and the Katz family shall be unusually linked together in My purposes for this hour." I smiled to myself at this unexpected word. "Well, Lord, if this is ever to take place, You'll have to work it out. Why, we don't even know one another yet!"

Charles and I walked through the large doors of the Seward College campus lounge. Across the room stood a tall, handsome man talking with some students. He looked up as he saw us come through the doors, excused himself from the conversation, and smilingly walked towards us. "You are obviously Charles Schmitt! Why, you could actually pass for my slightly *younger* brother. Say, what size coat do you wear? Imagine, we could even wear the same clothes."

"You even sound like one another when you preach," Gene laughingly commented.

And so we finally met Charles' look-alike. And with that initial meeting there began a series of events which were to change all of our lives.

"Dotty, what do you think of Art and Inger and the family moving to Dominion? Art believes that the Lord has given them the farm and land across from Dominion."

"But it's not even for sale!" I responded to Charles' question.

"Well, you know Art. If he feels the Lord has spoken to him, he'll boldly move into it." It was only a few months later that the Ben Israel Ministries purchased the farm and acreage directly across from Dominion.

During the past couple of years our friendship had definitely grown. We frequently found ourselves being invited to minister at the same conferences. And eventually Buck, Art, and Charles became the general overseers of the Dominion properties. Our children, being of similar ages, also developed a love and fondness for one another. (In fact, so committed were they to one another that when the Katz family visited us in Minnesota on one occasion, they even shared with us their chicken pox!)

Although Art and Charles looked similar in appearance, their temperaments were as different as day and night. Charles was a German Gentile from a strict fundamentalist background. Art was an American Jew from a very liberal background. What a tremendous opportunity to demonstrate practically the reality of the unity of the Body of Christ.

Having the two families in association at camp together has always been an experience! "Charles, don't you think some of your teaching tends to be a little sterile and plastic at times?"

"Rather that way than the erratic prophetic tendencies that come forth when you share, Arthur."

"Well, here we go again! Do you men ever think you'll agree on anything?" I exasperatedly interjected.

A small group of us were having a rather lively discussion in the main camp house called *Judah*. Sitting on the steps leading up to the loft was Inger, sewing on some

124

needlework. "You know, I think God is showing me something. I see a huge castle and it is protected by a strong chain. It is impossible to break the chain from the outside, but as one link continues to rub against the other a weakness is developed and it soon breaks from within."

"You're right, Inger! The world cannot pull us apart, but internal friction certainly can," Gene added.

"Look, we need to see *God's* view of this place and of our relationships," I observed. "If one Jew and one Gentile cannot get it together, how can we expect the whole church to do so? God is adding more and more Jewish believers to the Body of Christ, and we're not meant to splinter into a hundred different segments because we see things differently. Paul plainly declares that Jesus has broken down the middle wall of partition, and that from Jew and Gentile He has made one new man (Eph. 2:14-15). We're all committed to this vision of the restoration of His glorious church. Well, then, we better humble ourselves before one another, no matter how right we each think we are. The unity of the church begins here between two men of God, between two families, and then it includes more and more people!" I fervently pled, as I reiterated some of Charles' favorite end-time themes!

Hence once again God had spoken peace to us in the midst of our differences, and we were able to effectively pray together and stay together!

LaPorte, Minnesota—a mere dot on the map! And yet to this little speck of geography (where Dominion is located) have come thousands of believers not only from all over the country but also from all over the world. The grounds themselves are truly most beautiful, but the facilities were initially extremely limited. Camp Dominion was destined to expose any unnecessary dependence upon even the most normal comforts of the flesh. Three showers for anywhere between two hundred and four hundred people, outhouses, cold running water, and bunk beds which tested one's endurance—all these features worked towards ensuring the fact that the people who were with us were certainly intent upon seeking the Lord and His kingdom first (or else had no other way to get home from camp!). All of this greatly appealed to Arthur's more austere nature, and frequently Dominion has been called a Minnesota end-time kibbutz!

Nonetheless, concentrated corporate experiences of fellowship, worship, and anointed teaching have changed and transformed many hundreds of lives! "You know, Dotty, it's amazing what's happening. I'm actually preaching more and more Charles' message on God's glorious end-time church, and Charles is declaring more and more my message on Christ's suffering!" I didn't know whether to laugh or weep at Art's statement at the conclusion of our last camp for the summer. Abundant gratitude filled my heart as I walked across the now cherished grounds, feeling the already cooler August air blow refreshingly on my face.

Thank You, Father, for the Body of Christ!
Thank You for the richness we find in diversity.
Thank You that although our gifts, ministries,
and personalities are different, we are one in
Your Spirit.

24

Blessed Ruination

One thing have I desired of the Lord, that will I seek after; that I may dwell in the house of the Lord all the days of my life, to behold the beauty of the Lord, and to enquire in his temple.

(Ps. 27:4)

"My dear, the women miss you. Please, just come up to camp for the day and have a time of sharing with them."

"A time of sharing? Charles, do you realize how blown away I am right about now? I need to be ministered to, and not to minister!"

"Well then, come up and be ministered to, but just come up!" Charles persistently urged, as he called me one day from Camp Dominion.

I hung up the phone and went into the small white and pink bedroom to change the diaper of my seven-week-old beautiful baby daughter. I picked her up and held her close to me. "I love you, I love you, delightful Jenny Ann, but you have brought quite a change into Mommy's life." I stood in her room quietly weeping—both from exhaustion at having been up most of the night with her and also from not understanding what had been happening in my life the past ten months. My mind reflected back to the women's retreat at which Gwen, Sigi, and I spoke in Albert Lea, Minnesota.

"Dotty, what do you think of family planning?" one of

the gals asked me at the conclusion of an afternoon seminar taught by a Christian nurse.

"Well, I'm for it! In fact, Charles and I are very pleased with our two daughters. They are now almost eleven and eight years old, and it's great being able to take them more and more with us as we travel. Because of our involvement in ministry, and our very busy schedule, we feel our family is complete as it is," I confidently shared, totally oblivious to the fact that I was already a couple of weeks pregnant!

"Dotty, don't be so silly! How could we be having another child after all this time?" Charles looked at me partially amused—but partially alarmed too.

"My dear husband, this doesn't fit in with any of our plans but I know I'm pregnant!" I now began weeping rather profusely.

"Dotty, let's be a little rational about this whole thing."

"Rational, rational? I am thirty-seven years old! I'm just beginning to lose some weight! You're traveling so much in the ministry! Our house is continuously full of people! Our youngest daughter will be almost nine when the baby is born. Can I travel with you with a tiny baby?" I now cried all the harder.

"Dotty, Betty has been waiting to talk to you," Sue, our much loved secretary and friend, informed me as I dejectedly entered the downstairs office.

"Well, what did the doctor say?" she called after me, for I walked past her without saying a word. "Dotty, what about Betty?"

"I can't see anyone now," I cried, and ran up the stairs to the refuge of my bedroom.

"Dotty, Dotty, it will be OK. You know the Lord is in

control of our lives. Please stop crying! You must now act in the maturity you teach others about!"

"Don't you preach at me, Charles; I don't need you to tell me how I should act. Leave me alone, just leave me alone!" I sobbed while lying across the bed.

During the next three months I hardly recognized myself. I would cry at the slightest provocation, I was tired all the time, and I was scarcely speaking to the Lord. "You didn't even give me any warning about such a major change in my life. This is completely unexpected, Lord, and a little unfair at this late date. Boy, Your ways are sure confusing at times," I wept one morning while folding Charles' socks.

"Dotty, I'm not going to tell you what you already know. Just be assured that I'm praying for you. 'All things do work together for good to them that love God,' and I know that's true in your lives," Shirley warmly encouraged me over the phone.

"Thanks, Shirl, for being such a faithful friend to me these past twelve years," I quietly said over the phone. "Just knowing that you love me even in my dejected, unvictorious state helps."

"My dear, I'm concerned for you. I have never seen you like this. You know I deeply love you. There is no reason to overreact so. God is still on His throne," said Charles holding me close after one especially bad spell of depression.

What was wrong with me, anyway? Why couldn't I get a hold of myself? I cried to myself.

The ring of the phone pierced the silence of the living room in which I was dejectedly sitting. "Dotty, are you all right? I haven't been able to get you off my mind all

129

morning," Gene's voice softly spoke from the other end. "My dear friend, I know you are very familiar with this psalm, but the Lord keeps impressing me that He has a word for you from it. Please reread Psalm 139!" I hung up the phone. I well knew that psalm and wasn't too impressed that God had a word for me from it. But because I deeply respected Gene's walk with the Lord, I opened my Bible. The words almost jumped from the page as I read.

> For You did form my inward parts, You did knit me together in my mother's womb. I will confess and praise You, for You are fearfully wonderful, and for the awful wonder of my birth! Wonderful are Your works, and that my inner self knows right well. My frame was not hidden from You, when I was being formed in secret and intricately and curiously wrought (as if embroidered with various colors) in the depths of the earth [a region of darkness and mystery]. Your eyes saw my unformed substance, and in Your book all the days of my life were written, before ever they took shape, when as yet there was none of them. How precious and weighty also are Your thoughts to me, O God! How vast is the sum of them! (Ps. 139:13-17, Amplified)

"My daughter, I have chosen this child for Myself. I have a specific purpose for the life of this one being formed within you."

"O Lord, it's been so long since I experienced Your presence. I have been so lonesome for You. It's terrible having a controversy with You. Lord, forgive me for so resisting Your will. O Lord, I'm so homesick for Your presence, I can hardly stand it. O Lord, forgive me for my stubbornness and for my angry thoughts. Please, Lord, restore to me the joy of Your salvation."

The Lord's presence filled Charles' little study as I

knelt at the big rocking chair. "Lord, Your will be done; Your will be done. And I declare Your will to be good, perfect, and acceptable." A weight fell from me that night, and slowly I began to experience again the joy of His presence.

"Dotty, we really believe the Lord is going to give you a son," said Gisela one day.

"Yes, I'm sensing that too," I answered. "After all, it would seem most logical that after these many years He would now complete our family in this way. I've gotten many letters from folks everywhere who likewise feel that the baby I'm carrying is a son," I happily reported to Gisela (who had also just recently had hers and Morrie's third child).

I looked at the clock: 2:30 A.M. I lay wide awake. The last of the leaders' wives had left our home about 12:15 A.M. Charles hadn't returned from being with all the men at the chapel until after 1:00 A.M. I returned from the bathroom and looked at him. He was sound asleep! At 2:45, I knew I had better awaken him.

"Charles, Charles, it's time!"

By 3:25 A.M. Charles and I were in the delivery room together. At 3:38 A.M. our nine-pound baby was quickly and easily delivered.

"Well, well, it looks as if the Schmitts are destined to raise girls. You have a big baby girl!" Doctor Erickson informed us.

"Praise the Lord," I spontaneously responded, and yet Charles and I looked at one another in bewilderment. I had been so sure this would be a boy.

The first time I held our beautiful daughter I experienced such an overwhelming sense of God's grace to us as a family that I wept. Lavona's statement to me during one evening while Charles and I (then in my eighth month of pregnancy) were attending the Catholic charismatic prayer meeting at St. Joseph's, flooded my mind: "Dorothy, the Lord must love you and your family so very much to give you the gift of this precious child." Charles chose the name of Jenny Ann. Jenny, in the Hebrew, means grace of God, and Ann means gracious one. How very appropriate! For in her we were receiving a double portion of His grace.

Yet once home from the hospital, the questions persisted. I knew all the traditional explanations of our desires coloring what we think He is saying, of not seeing the total picture, of His timing being involved in the fulfillment of certain prophecies, etc., etc. Still, there was something of a spiritual numbness on the inside of me: How could I have been so wrong in interpreting His voice?

I drove to camp that day in obedience to Charles' phone call. Yes, it was good to worship with God's people again! We began singing Psalm 84:

> How lovely is Thy dwelling place, O Lord of Hosts,
> My soul longs and yearns for Your courts;
> And my heart and flesh sing for joy to the living God.
> One day in Thy presence is far better to me than gold,
> Or to live my whole life somewhere else.
> And I would rather be a doorkeeper in Your house
> Than to take my fate upon myself.
> You are my Sun and my Shield,
> You're my Lover from the start,
> And the highway to Your City
> Runs through my heart.

As we sang the last two lines, the tears began to stream down my face. I stood with my hands raised to the Lord. Such a love welled up within me for my God. As we sang this song again and again, His anointing gently moved among us.

"Ruined, Lord, ruined! That's exactly what I am! I am ruined for anything, or anyone else, but You. No matter what I do or do not understand about Your ways, we are stuck with each other. You have become the very joy of my life; without You I am and have nothing. O Father, I lay my questions all before You, and humbly worship You."

So what do we do when we make mistakes, or when we misinterpret His leadings? Well, we own up to it, and honestly say, Lord, I was wrong! We don't try to rationalize or "spiritualize" our misinterpretations. We simply lay aside our own understandings, and trust *Him*. How very pertinent Prov. 3:5-6 has become to me: "Trust in the Lord with all thine heart; and lean not unto thine own understanding. In all thy ways acknowledge *him*, and he shall direct thy paths." In His time He will perhaps supply answers; but meanwhile, being wrong once in a while can be a healthy experience, for it keeps one humble and a little less likely to judge another when he or she makes mistakes. How liberating to know that "the Lord God is a sun and shield: the Lord will give grace and glory: *no good thing will he withhold from them that walk uprightly*" (Ps. 84:11).

Hallelujah, Father, for the revelation of Your-self, which is the *answer to life. You are* love. *And everything that comes from Your hand is a result of Your love for us. Thank You that You write Your name upon our hearts, and that we're then wonderfully ruined for anything else. Father, You are that which we desire, and which we will seek after.*

25

Victory in the Midst of Devastation

*He will swallow up death in victory; and the
Lord God will wipe away tears from off all
faces.*

(Isa. 25:8)

Although the December Florida sun shone warmly
upon me, my insides were becoming increasingly numb
with the shock of what was happening. While I was
kneeling—partly on the concrete and partly on the
lawn—there lay next to me one of the most important
persons in my life. As I helplessly knelt beside him,
instinctively I knew I was facing the strongest and most
bitter enemy I would ever face: death!

It initially was totally unreal! Why, he had just made
breakfast for us all. Only minutes before, he had gone
out to mow the lawn which grew so rapidly under the
heat of the Florida sun. Hadn't he, mere seconds
before, stopped the lawn mower to talk and laugh with
his three granddaughters? They were always calling to
"Opa" for something. "Oh, no, my God, this is
impossible! This is not really happening! My God, I
love this man! God, please . . ." But even as I knelt
there praying, numbly watching life ebb from this
dearly loved frame which had just suffered a sudden
massive heart attack, I somehow knew God's ap-

pointed hour had come for my precious dad!

"Dotty, now don't cry. We had a wonderful summer with you all. We'll see you at Christmas time "

"I know, Dad, but you and Mom mean so much to me, I don't like to see you leave." I gave them both another hug, and watched them pull out of our driveway in Grand Rapids.

It had been a great summer in that year of 1976. My parents were delighted with their granddaughters, and the newest addition especially brought joy to them.

"Dotty, what exactly do you find to talk about to all those women?" Dad had asked me, as he, Mom, and I sat around the table preparing fresh string beans for the freezer. I had recently returned from a weekend retreat in Missouri.

"You didn't know you had such a 'mouthy' daughter, did you?" I teased.

"Well, you sure didn't get it from me," he laughed, while fondly glancing at my mom.

"You know, I happen to have one of the tapes from this weekend. Want to listen?" I put on the tape of a message in which I had shared with the women how the relationship with my earthly father helped prepare me for the revelation of my heavenly Father. Tears filled my dad's large brown eyes as he listened. I went over to where he was sitting and gave him a hug. "It's true, Dad; your love for us and your kindness to us helped me better understand the love and kindness of my heavenly Father."

The girls could hardly wait for Christmas. "Only ten days more! Whoopie!" Dianna could be heard laughing in her room as she marked off another day on her calendar.

At last the morning came for us to fly down to Fort Lauderdale as a family.

We had already enjoyed a happy ten days together. "Dotty, Dotty, I can't believe this happened so fast," Charles kept saying while holding my mom and myself in his arms. All three of us stood together, holding one another, weeping. Dad died about nine-thirty in the morning, five days before Christmas. The remainder of the day we walked numbly about making the necessary arrangements. Everything was rather unreal to me.

Even in the midst of the terrible inner pain and turmoil I was experiencing, the words of Paul were giving me a strength I had not known before: "So when this corruptible shall have put on incorruption, and this mortal shall have put on immortality, then shall be brought to pass the saying that is written, Death is swallowed up in victory . . . But thanks be to God which gives us the victory through our Lord Jesus Christ" (1 Cor. 15:54, 57). Jesus Christ, the Victor, has conquered this great and terrible avenger! This is the great unalterable Hope of our Christian faith.

In those moments, on that traumatic and painful morning, I knew that He to whom I had committed my life some twenty-five years previously was in very fact the great Rock under my feet. And strangely enough, as I came face to face with this horrible enemy, the fear of it left me. Afterwards, while reflecting on this, I thought about the truth of Heb. 2:14-15: "Forasmuch then as the children are partakers of flesh and blood, he also himself likewise took part of the same; that through death he might destroy him that had the power of death, that is, the devil; and deliver them who through fear of death were all their lifetime subject to bondage."

That night I went alone outside to sit a while. The

Florida air felt warm. I looked up, and was impressed with the brightness of so many stars. I wanted to pray. But the words stuck in my throat. In years past I had so thoroughly enjoyed addressing God as my Father, but now I couldn't even speak the word. It hurt too much. Eventually, though, through the tears, the words falteringly came: "Lord, thanks for Your understanding during these days. Thank You that You too were 'a man of sorrows and acquainted with grief.' Lord, it's going to take a little time before I can again freely say 'Father' to You. What a comfort to know You understand." It was then that deep within me I heard the still and gentle voice of the God whom I had grown to love and depend on during the past years.

"You know that *I* will never die. Your life with Me as your Father can only increase, never decrease. You need never fear losing the uniqueness of your relationship with Me. I am always there, and I will never fail you."

Somehow I sensed that my earthly dad would have wanted, more than anything else, for me, his beloved daughter, to be richer in spirit and not poorer, because of his transition from this life to the next. On that night of sorrow I also experienced the love of my heavenly Father in an entirely new and deeper dimension.

The tears still periodically come as I recall the different experiences with this very tender and giving man. Yet there is also a new perception of Paul's statement in 1 Thess. 4:13, "But I would not have you to be ignorant, brethren, concerning them which are asleep, that ye sorrow not, even as others which have no hope." Jesus Christ has brought to this earth *hope*. It is not wishful thinking to believe that there is more to life than this earthly existence. It is the clear declaration of the life, death, and resurrection of our Lord Jesus Christ. He has completely triumphed over all which the great enemy of our soul has attempted to do!

In less than a year my father-in-law was also to die, so that both our mothers were now suddenly widowed. With both our fathers' deaths, our mothers became even more dear to us. Now with greater perception, I appreciated God's view of the widow: "The Lord will destroy the house of the proud: but he will establish the border of the widow" (Prov. 15:25).

Looking back over the events of 1976 has at times left me stunned. The stark realities of our earthly existence became ever more clear to me during that year. One month I experienced the joy and excitement of watching my baby breathe her first breath and sound her first cry; seven months later I knelt next to my beloved dad, watching him breathe his last breath and utter his last sound!

The issues of life and death! How pertinent the statement of the poet: "To every thing there is a season, and a time to every purpose under the heaven: a time to be born, and a time to die" (Eccles. 3:1-2). God has put eternity into our hearts. We were not created to die but to live—and to live creatively and abundantly!

With such contrasts of life and death so plainly before me, I could only worship at the feet of Him who holds the keys to both life and death. How foolish of us to waste precious time indulging in negative attitudes and harboring unforgiving spirits. How absurd to walk in the ways of a decadent world system and cling to worldly possessions and pleasures which are so very fleeting. And how very expedient to live in the purpose for which we have been created. As Jesus himself explained, "My meat is to do the will of him that sent me, and to finish his work" (John 4:34).

Father, never again shall I use that address to You without also thanking You for my earthly dad whom You gave to me for these thirty-eight years. Know also, Father, that I yield my life afresh to You—with renewed determination and consecration, that Your triumphant kingdom may shortly be established on this very weary and needy earth. Maranatha, Lord, do come quickly.

26

Unto the Uttermost Parts

Ask of me, and I shall give thee the heathen for thine inheritance, and the uttermost parts of the earth for thy possession.

(Ps. 2:8)

"Girls, hurry up, hurry up! Today's the day! Your dad will soon be home!" I excitedly called to the girls. "Oh, how I wish the airport weren't a four-hour drive for us."

"Mom, you'd think Dad was gone for a year rather than a month, the way you're carrying on," Laura teased, as she, Dianna, and I got into the car.

We were held up in traffic, so we were a little late to the Minneapolis/St. Paul airport. I felt like a school girl. Charles had been in India and Sri Lanka. It had felt to us as though he were at the end of the world—no phone calls, and only a few letters! "Hurry, the plane should be arriving already," I called to the girls as we ran through the airport terminal.

"I think I see him," Dianna enthusiastically shouted, at the same time hopping up and down.

"No, silly, that's not him. But I think I see his shoes," Laura more calmly interjected.

"No, that's not him either!"

"Stewardess, there must be someone else in that plane! My husband's on that flight."

"Sorry, but everyone's out. Perhaps he missed the flight."

My heart sank. I couldn't remember when I had been so filled with expectation and anticipation. "Oh no," the girls sighed.

"Mrs. Charles Schmitt, please pick up the white extension phone for Northwest Orient Airlines."

"Hello, hello!"

"Your husband, Mrs. Schmitt, flew in late from England. He will arrive in three hours on the next flight from New York."

As we sat down in the busy lounge to wait, a Scripture passage flooded my mind. I turned in my Amplified Bible to where I thought it was; yes, Isa. 30:18: "And therefore the Lord [earnestly] waits—expectant, looking and long-ing—to be gracious to you, and therefore He lifts Himself up that He may have mercy on you and show loving-kindness to you; for the Lord is a God of justice. Blessed . . . are all those who [earnestly] wait for Him, who expect and look and long for Him [for His victory, His favor, His love, His peace, His joy and His matchless, unbroken companionship]."

"Even as you have waited for Charles, so have I waited for My people. How often My Bride feels she's waiting for Me, but I tell you that it is I, the Bridegroom, who waits, eagerly longing for her companionship."

I reread the verse. "Thank You, Lord, thank You, Lord, for that illumination of Your heart! Thank You that You wait and long to be gracious to us."

While watching the myriads of people coming and going, I smiled with gratitude and fulfillment. It had been a good time while Charles was gone, although there were some very trying days. Jenny had become quite ill with a high fever and ear infection. But I was surrounded with God's family when I had to rush her to the hospital. Although Morrie was in India with Charles, Gisela and the rest of her family were living with us; their home—which was partially destroyed by a fire—had not yet been completed. How vital the family of God is! Gisela and I thoroughly enjoyed being together for these weeks. In fact, we needed one another more than ever before since our husbands were laboring together in India.

"Dotty, how do you stand Charles' being away from home so much? Don't you get lonesome for him?" one of the sisters in our fellowship sympathetically asked me. "And what about all the things which come up while he's gone. I simply don't know how you handle it all."

Without her realizing it, her statements further contributed to my pangs of self-pity. Recently I had been feeling sorry for myself. I thought of all we had to sacrifice for being in the ministry. One afternoon while I was reading the Gospel of Mark, the Lord spoke to me: "Jesus said, Truly, I tell you, there is no one who has given up and left house or brothers or sisters or mother or father or children or lands, for My sake and for the Gospel, who will not receive a hundred times as much now in this time, houses and brothers and sisters and mothers and children and lands, with persecutions, and in the age to come eternal life" (Mark 10:29-30, Amplified).

"My daughter, I desire to straighten out some of your crooked thinking. Rather than feel sorry for yourself, you are to rejoice in the privilege I am giving you to so labor in My kingdom. Do you think you can outgive Me? Do you not realize that I always return to My people a hundredfold in this life and in the life to come? My daughter, has not your life been enriched in every way?"

I knelt in repentance before the Lord. "Lord, thank You for exposing my foolish self-centeredness. And thank You that Your grace is sufficient for my every need. Thank You that it is a privilege to give my husband to You to serve You wherever You call him. And yes, Lord, thank You that our marriage is one of the richest I have seen. Why, his being away has actually strengthened our relationship. Thank You that I can pray for him. Thank You that when he fulfills what he has been created to do, he is even a better husband and father. Thank You, Father, for all the people in India and Sri Lanka who will be in the kingdom because Charles was there! Praise Your name, that You have chosen us to so serve You. And Lord, thank You for the many times I have been able to travel and minister with him. Thank You for the vision of the restoration of Your church, which burns in both our hearts."

As I prayed, I remembered back to when we lived in our mobile home in Cohasset. Charles had always had world maps on the study wall. On one occasion I overheard him cry, "Lord Jesus, Lord Jesus, will what I have seen revealed in Your Word ever come to pass? Will Your church manifest Your manifold wisdom and power in this generation? Dear Lord, when will I see Your promise fulfilled? How long, Lord, how long?"

Hearing him so call on the Lord, I thought of the verse which he had frequently claimed since we were teenagers: "From the rising of the sun even unto the going down of the same my name shall be great among the Gentiles; and in every place incense shall be offered unto my name, and a pure offering: for my name shall be great among the heathen, saith the Lord of hosts" (Mal. 1:11)

There was no question of God's moving by His Spirit in this country. Hundreds o groups of believers were springing up all over. They were meeting in homes, schools, church basements, anywhere that could accommodate a group of people. We were also finding similar events taking place in other countries where we had been—Jamaica, Canada, Puerto Rico, and England. There were beginning signs of the outpouring of His Spirit in Germany and Switzerland. And perhaps closest to our hearts of all the places we had been, in the land of Israel. Mercy drops were indeed beginning to fall on the natural seed of David—with a promise of more to come!

"Mom, come on, it's almost time," said Dianna, running over to where I was sitting. I had been deep in thought when the girls returned from the gift shop.

"Well, OK! The last one at the gate has to treat us to an ice-cream cone."

"Oh, Mom, what are people going to think?" Laura laughed as all three of us raced to Gate Three.

Finally, Charles walked down the ramp. A little stunned, I looked at his recently grown black-and-white beard, and at his thinner frame. "Why, my dear, you've lost at least ten pounds," I cried as we all three ran into his outstretched arms. And there we all stood, weeping and laughing at the same time. "O my dear Charles, it is so good to have you home again."

I received back from India a changed husband. Even more fervently than before, there burned within him the vision of the glorious church which God was restoring among all the nations!

Thank You, Father, for moving all over the earth by Your Spirit. Thank You that men and women are being born daily into Your kingdom. And thank You for the privilege of being co-laborers with You in the bringing forth of Your purposes in this hour.

27

Time to Be Replanted

What man is he that feareth the Lord? him shall he teach in the way that he shall choose. (Ps.25:12)

It was already 11:20 P.M. I wondered to whom Charles was talking for so long a period of time.

I finished reading the last chapter of Colossians from the Phillips translation, and was just about to turn off the light when Charles came into the bedroom. He sat on our recently purchased waterbed, and merely gave me a long amused look.

"Well, what's up? Who were you talking to?"

"Dotty, I don't know what you're going to think about this! I'm even a little shocked about it myself."

"Charles, please; you can't keep me hanging there. What is it?"

"Well, what would you think if we moved from Grand Rapids?"

"I'm open to going to only one place, Washington, D.C."

"What made you say that?"

"Why, I really don't know, it sort of just popped out!"

"My mystical wife!" Charles laughed.

"Well, my dear husband, tell me what you are thinking. Do you realize we have lived here for fifteen years? I really like it here. I enjoy my home, and love the people. Like--where would we move to?"

Numerous questions were asked and answered during those next very busy and exciting months of change. In His will we soon found ourselves back on the East Coast. Many were the new friends we found and loved.

In the providence of God this major move back to the East Coast would see wrought in our lives the most significant changes yet. The psalmist describes most accurately the faithfulness of our God to us as individuals and as a family: "Because he hath sent his love upon me, therefore will I deliver him: I will set him on high, because he hath known my name. He shall call upon me, and I will answer him: I will be with him in trouble; I will deliver him, and honour him" (Ps. 91:14, 15).

For me personally the move east was accompanied at one juncture by some of the deepest turmoil I have ever known. But this was graciously overshadowed by the joy of coming to know the love of the Lord even more.

Growth involves changes, and change can be painful. But when our Father is in control of our lives, the change brings forth delightful results. Recently, as we were driving back home from Minnesota, from our beloved Camp Dominion, I reached out simply to hold Charles' hand. We were driving through some of the most beautiful pastoral country side of Wisconsin. "You know, my dear, the Lord has brought us into a most incredibly wide experience of His Church over these past years. It's almost hard for me to imagine all the doors of fellowship and ministry He has opened up to us. What an amazingly faithful God we serve!"

Charles glanced at me smiling pensively, "The Church is far wider and greater than we had ever imagined. And more than anything else, I see that we are to be a totally redemptive and restorative community."

"Why does it seem that we learn the ways of mercy, forgiveness, and kindness only after we ourselves have been in such need of them?" I mused. Both Charles and I settled back into a peaceful, thoughtful silence. How rich had been our time at Dominion! I felt nurtured emotionally and spiritually, for we as a family were among some of our closest friends, some of whom we have known for more than twenty years. These friendships were tested and tried, but by God's grace they have endured and have today become one of life's most enriching experiences for us.

As the miles continued to pass, a growing anticipation filled my heart. "You know, Charles, Immanuel's Church is one of the most vital groups I've ever been involved in.* It's hard to imagine that such growth has taken place within these past few years."

"There's no question that these dear people have won a very special place in our hearts. I remember the word the Lord gave us a couple of years ago,'...I called upon the Lord...the Lord answered me, and set me in a large place'" (Ps. 117:5). I pondered the words "a large place." In all the dealings and prunings of God, His objective is always for our good, always to bring us into "a large place."

---

*In the fall of 1983 Immanuel's Church was sovereignly raised up by our Lord Jesus Christ to help serve the purposes of God in the Baltimore-Washington, D.C. area. From a small group of a dozen believers meeting in Charles' and Dotty's living room, Immanuel's Church grew over 8 years to become twelve hundred in number, with a developing outreach and influence that now stretches across the country and around the world.

Thank you, Father, that you are the joy of life. Thanks also that you lead Your people with Your own voice. And, Father, thank You that when You prune our lives, it is always so that we may become even more fruitful in Your vineyard.

Epilogue

"It is the blessing of the Lord that makes rich and He adds no sorrow to it." (Pro. 10:22)

Through all the testings and the triumphs, by His grace, we have as a family been enriched in the awesome knowledge of Himself, and in the grateful enjoyment of all of His blessings.

Along with our teenage Jenny and dear Nana Schmitt, Charles and I recently moved out into the country, complete with the crowing of roosters and the mooing of cows just 20 minutes from Immanuel's Worship Center. It is wonderfully beyond our expectations!

As soon as Laura and George sell their present house, they will hopefully move in with us while they are in the process of building their new home. (Our son-in-law George has shown his expertise not only as a computer engineer, but also in "house building" as he finishes working on our new house). Laura continues to excel in her computer engineering, having also taken on consulting in addition to her regular job. Dianna and Scott live in Wheaton, Illinois, where they are both very busy in their very demanding individual jobs -- Dianna, on the administrative staff at a nursing home, and Scott in the challenging family manufacturing business. Our dear Jenny is now 16, and drives all around our new neighborhood. She worked at Immanuel's summer camp and continues to thrill us with her love for the Lord. My aunt lives but a few minutes from us in a retirement home. Some of the richest times for the Schmitts is when the whole family is able to gather together around the dining room table! We increasingly treasure our family and the blessings of our relationships with one another.

All these experiences overflow into our life together at Immanuel's Church, which is our wider family in God! I am now full-time on our pastoral staff (complete with my own office and secretary) and find that my heart is full of love for the many folks the Lord has joined to Immanuel's. In the midst of family and church, I still travel, ministering to the wider Body of Christ. Because of our continued growth as a local church, Charles has chosen, with few exceptions, to concentrate primarily on teaching, pastoring, and leading this most challenging and delightful growing congregation!

The Schmitts have been greatly blessed and enriched in every way over these past years, and we can only encourage every one of you to remain faithful and obedient to the great Shepherd of our souls. He is Lord of the valleys as well as the Lord of the mountains.

O Father, standing on the sundeck of our new home, the sun has just burst through the clouds! I am again reminded that the greatest experience of my whole life is experiencing the warmth of Your love. And in turn Your love has taught me how to love You more. How to accept and enjoy myself, and how to love and enjoy others. Thank You, Father, that the most incredible power upon earth is Your love--and thank You that Your love never fails. No matter how dark the clouds, nothing can separate us from your healing, delivering love! And thank You, Father, that it is an utter delight to be Your daughter and that You are going to have for Your Son a beautiful Bride without spot or wrinkle, one who wears combat boots!

(And soon to be published -- Dotty's new book: "The Bride Wears Combat Boots!")